WHOA,
MY BOSS IS NAKED!

WHOA,
MY BOSS IS NAKED!

A CAREER BOOK FOR PEOPLE WHO
WOULD NEVER BE CAUGHT DEAD
READING A CAREER BOOK

Jake Greene

CURRENCY   DOUBLEDAY

New York London Toronto Sydney Auckland

A CURRENCY BOOK
PUBLISHED BY DOUBLEDAY

Published in the United States by Doubleday, an imprint of
The Doubleday Broadway Publishing Group, a division of
Random House, Inc., New York.
www.currencybooks.com

CURRENCY is a trademark of Random House, Inc., and
DOUBLEDAY is a registered trademark of Random House, Inc.

All trademarks are the property of their respective companies.

Book design by Michael Collica

Library of Congress Cataloging-in-Publication Data
Greene, Jake.
  Whoa, my boss is naked!: a career book for people who
would never be caught dead reading a career book / Jake
Greene.—1st ed.
    p.   cm.
1. Career development. 2. Vocational guidance. 3. Success in
business. 4. Young adults—Employment. I. Title.

  HF5381.G85587 2008
  650.1—dc22

                                                2007023022

ISBN: 978-0-385-52337-0

PRINTED IN THE UNITED STATES OF AMERICA

SPECIAL SALES
Currency Books are available at special discounts for bulk
purchases for sales promotions or premiums. Special editions,
including personalized covers, excerpts of existing books, and
corporate imprints, can be created in large quantities for
special needs. For more information, write to Special Markets,
Currency Books, specialmarkets@randomhouse.com.

10 9 8 7 6 5 4 3 2 1

First Edition

For Sarah

Contents

WHOA,
MY BOSS IS NAKED!

Introduction

THIS IS *NOT* ANOTHER "CORPORATE TOOLS FOR CORPORATE TOOLS" HANDBOOK.

THIS IS *NOT* another "Corporate Tools for Corporate Tools" handbook. There are no bogus guarantees or dopey "Twelve Steps to Prosperity" contained inside. In the event that you were hoping for something more along the lines of, say, *Seven Elements of a Supremely Powerful Leader, Thirteen Ways to Revolutionize Your Career–and Your Life!,* or *Ten Habits of Fully Fulfilled People,* I'm afraid you're going to be pretty disappointed. Furthermore, reading this book will not make you smarter, wealthier, or better looking. Don't get me wrong, there's a lot of useful stuff in here about how to land a good job and make some noise once you've got it, but if you're a lazy slob ... well, let's just say it's neither my intent nor my place to wean you off Cheetos and "Celebreality." It *is* my intent, however, to help you get a tighter grip on the professional world without losing your identity and becoming a Corporate Tool. More on this in a moment.

This *is* a book of career advice for the pop culture generation. I'm talking about those of us who grew up with music videos, the Internet, and reality television. We were there when Jeremy spoke in class, Kanye dropped out, and Donna Martin graduated. Throughout our formative years in the '80s and '90s, we learned important lessons from pop culture professors, and I see no reason that can't continue as we shape our professional lives.

You'll find this book full of examples, anecdotes, and stories pulled from the last twenty years of pop culture—from movies like *Anchorman* and *Clueless*, TV shows like *Survivor* and *Project Runway*, and from musicians like Metallica and Hanson (don't worry, you'll understand that last one when you get there). Who knew that watching Steve Carell fail with the ladies could help you communicate at work, or that *Mean Girls* and *Donnie Brasco* could help you get a life outside the office?

CORPORATE TOOLS DEFINED

So, what exactly is a Corporate Tool? Unfortunately, there is no precise definition of the term. Social scientists, business leaders, and bartenders at Applebee's haven't been able to reach a consensus. To me, Corporate Tools are professionals without perspective. They are blindly loyal to their organizations and bring a "Thank you, sir, may I have another?" mentality to work each day. They are so severely indoctrinated into a given professional culture that they lose touch with life outside the office. Much like the royal advisors in *The Emperor's New Clothes*, Corporate Tools strut around town with their chests puffed out, praising the emperor's (or the boss's) style in defiance of their own senses. In other words, they own a lot of Dockers but they don't wear the pants, ya dig?

Corporate Tools don't usually like their jobs. Oh sure, they'll tell you that they do, but it's obvious that they're full of it. If they liked their jobs, they wouldn't go on and on about the material rewards they earn as opposed to the work they do. They wouldn't get so defensive when people utter even moderately negative comments about their employers. And they wouldn't keep saying, "How cool would it be if I could do *that* for a living," every time they watched *CSI, Iron Chef,* or HGTV. Corporate Tools hope that by convincing others they love what they're doing they will come closer to convincing themselves that they aren't stuck in jobs that are utterly uninspiring.

Here are some additional behaviors and signs that might help you recognize Corporate Tools when you come across them in the wild:

- Corporate Tools overestimate the importance of their jobs by a factor of ten.
  Example: "If nobody sold pharmaceuticals, people wouldn't get the medicine they needed and everyone would DIE."
- Corporate Tools proudly display motivational artwork ("Successories") in their workspaces.
  Example: I recently saw one piece that showed an eagle flying in the mountains. The caption read: "DARE TO SOAR: Your attitude almost always determines your altitude." I immediately threw up in my mouth.
- Corporate Tools proudly display electronic devices on their beltlines à la Batman.
  Example: I particularly like the people who have multiple Blackberry clips to match different outfits.
- Corporate Tools swear by "mottoes" and "credos" that one might see in an ad for GloboGym or hear on reruns of *Kung Fu: The Legend Continues.*
  Example: "Adversity reveals strength."
- Corporate Tools find ways to use professional lingo in casual conversation.
  Example: "Bill, our room is a mess and your buddies left beer cans all over the apartment. Have you forgotten all the BDPs (Best Demonstrated Practices) we talked about?"

- Corporate Tools frequently add uncomfortable suffixes, left over from their fraternity days, onto the ends of their colleagues' names.
  Example: "Jake-*er*," "Kell-*dawg*," and "Boone-*meister*."
- Corporate Tools take travel points *way* too seriously.
  Example: Don't be surprised when the fellas throw a party for Janice at Chili's when she goes platinum with Marriott or joins the Hertz #1 Club Gold. High fives and Southwestern Egg Rolls for everyone!
- Corporate Tools quote *Wall Street, Boiler Room,* and *Working Girl* without irony.
  Example: "They say money can't buy happiness? Look at the fucking smile on my face. Ear to ear, baby." (Ben Affleck in *Boiler Room*)

Now, despite what your microbrew-drinking, indie band–listening, track pants–wearing, burnout roommates might say, playing a role in Corporate America DOES NOT make you a Corporate Tool by default. I personally know too many successful, inspired, and generally happy people who work corporate gigs to claim otherwise. The fact is, there are way more cool people working corporate gigs than there are Tools. What's more, there are plenty of Tools honing their craft *outside* of Corporate America. Artists, lawyers, nurses, bartenders, and circus performers are not immune. Ya'll are as much at risk as the rest of us, so pay attention.

In addition to offering advice about interviewing, networking, and handling your business at the office, this book aims to steer you away from the clichéd life and lingo of Corporate Tools. Away from "value-added paradigm shifts" and cheesy people who want to "touch base off-line." Away from the "synergies," "home runs," and "low-hanging fruit" lurking just "outside the box." Yes, the evil forces of the Dork Side are lurking behind every water cooler and color copier, but you will learn to recognize and repel them. And when you look up from your desk to see a puffed-up Corporate Tool high-fiving and name-dropping his way around the office, you will have the confidence and courage to boldly proclaim: "Whoa, my boss is naked!"

So what makes me qualified to write this book? That's a fair question. After all, I'm just a no-name punk (like many of you) carving out my place in the professional world. I am neither old nor rich. I don't run a Fortune 100 company or a Fortune 100,000 company. But I do know how to land a job, and get ahead once I'm there. I have studied business culture professionally and academically for the past decade. I have done business in all four corners of the country and held positions in health care, retail development, advertising, movie promotion, and real estate investment. I also hold a master's degree from Stanford in sociology, focusing on organizations, business, and the economy (though most of my friends are more impressed with my "certificate of achievement" from the Minnesota School of Bartending).

More important, I don't need to rack my brain to remember what life was like before I had three administrative assistants and stock options. The advice and anecdotes in this book come straight from the street, from twenty-first-century twentysomethings.

You may have heard some of this advice before. I'm not out to pretend I've developed some groundbreaking psycho-economic theory or discovered a secret Harry Potter–style spell for success (*"Fulloshitronium!"*). At the end of the day, my goal is to help you land a good job if you need one, and help you get ahead if you already have one.

PART ONE

Ain't Nothin' to It but to Do It

LOOKING FOR A CAREER THAT'S INSPIRING AND IN VOGUE? FREE YOUR MIND AND YOUR BUTT WILL FOLLOW.

Get Up, Get Out, and Do Something

FOLD UP THE FUTON. IT'S TIME TO GO GET YOUR HANDS DIRTY.

HAVE YOU EVER watched the same episode of *The Real World* three times in a single week? Nothing changes. J.T. always gets arrested on the beach for mouthing off to the bicycle cops, and Lavender still breaks down when forced to confront her addictions to sex and flavored lip gloss...yet you still can't muster up the motivation to change the channel. Your sweatpants stink, the Wheat Thins are stale, and there's a chopstick caught between one of the couch cushions and your thigh. It's been poking you for the last four hours, so you've gotten used to the discomfort. It's 1:30 p.m. on a Wednesday....

If I just described your typical afternoon, you should be aware that you may have come down with a not-so-rare case of post-graduation paralysis, referred to in select medical circles as *Midas-itis*. Midas-itis is a serious psychological disorder that infects millions of twentysomethings every year and is especially common among young people with multiple interests who view themselves as "gifted" or "talented." The condition is characterized by massive swelling in the entitlement/unrealistic-expectation sector of the brain causing victims to believe that they should only pursue "golden" career opportunities.* Unable to quickly identify such utopian employment environments and unwilling to sell themselves short, infected parties inevitably grow depressed and recoil from the real world. Symptoms include (but are not limited to) multiple unfinished movie scripts, untouched graduate school applications, interactive gaming addiction, and/or excessive VH1 viewing.

I caught Midas-itis as a student in Silicon Valley right around Y2K. The Internet was in full boom, and it seemed as though every time I picked up a newspaper there was a picture of some kid (usually not much older than I) who had just turned a computer program into a multimillion-dollar start-up company. Google, eBay, and Napster were close enough to touch, and a constant reminder of the riches awaiting computer science graduates. Naturally, I convinced myself I should study computers, start a dot-com where roller blades and baseball hats were allowed in the office, cash in on a godzillion-dollar IPO (initial public offering), and then ride off into the sunset in a Beemer so tricked out you'd swear it could fly. Only problem: I sucked at computer science. I am not using the term "sucked" lightly, either. I don't have a single iota of technical talent in my body. I peaked as a computer scientist in elementary school playing "The Oregon Trail" on the Apple IIGS (I was particularly adept at fording rivers and hunting). To add insult to injury, the Internet bubble burst a few months later thereby obliterating my already fading dot-com dream. Even so, I naively assumed that another wave of opportunity would simply wash up on my doorstep, so I waited on the couch and proceeded to lose three months of my life to *Behind the Music* and PlayStation.

---

*Midas is a character in Greek mythology who turned everything he touched into gold (as opposed to the muffler shop). This is the first and last academic reference in this book, I swear.

Luckily, Midas-itis is not difficult to cure. In fact, all you have to do is get over yourself and get off the couch. Get up, get out, and do something! Quit imagining what the working world *should* look like and start experiencing what it does look like. There's a reason that they call it a "job *search*." You need to actively hunt. Will you find a job that allows you to change the world, make millions, and unlock your full range of creative abilities right out of the gate? Doubtful, but so what? Nobody starts at the top. Even Harvard MBAs have to fetch coffee once in a while.

C'mon, would you rather spend the next year out in the world showcasing your talents and figuring out what drives your ambition, or in your parents' basement trying to figure out which contestant in the "Showcase Showdown" will win a Broyhill bedroom set or drive off in a brand-new Chevy Malibu? Don't worry about selling out your dreams or wasting your "unique" talents in a windowless cubicle for the next thirty years. The concept of the thirty-year fixed career track expired back when Alex Trebek was still hosting *Classic Concentration*. So get off your ass and get moving. Ain't nothin' to it but to do it.

The Reason Most Bands Suck

YOU NEED TO "COMMIT TO A SOUND" BEFORE YOU CAN GET SIGNED.

FACT: *MOST BANDS suck*. For every chart-topping Coldplay or Red Hot Chili Peppers, there are thousands of awful bands polluting the stages, bars, and college radio stations of this great country. That is not to say that most bands can't keep a beat, get along, or stay sober. No, most bands suck because they refuse to commit to a sound and allow themselves to be defined. In striving to dodge convention (and evaluation), these bands end up with set lists that sound like they were lifted off a schizophrenic's iPod. They might open with a jazzy "composition," follow up with a Jack Johnson–style bonfire number, and then revive a monster ballad cover, such as Bon Jovi's "Wanted Dead or Alive." In the end, all six people who happened to catch the show at Jean Claude's Coffee Cafe will walk away confused and upset, totally unable to qualify what they've just listened to. It doesn't matter whether or not these bands are talented; all the skill and ability in the world won't do them any good until they learn to define their sound. In this regard, the professional world is a lot like the music world. If you refuse to "commit to a sound," you won't get signed either.

Want a job in finance? Then you're going to have to commit to becoming a "finance person." You can begin by watching CNBC and checking out *The Wall Street Journal.* Or maybe you'd rather be a travel writer? Then you need to start traveling and (you guessed it) writing. Sounds simple, right? Surprisingly, many of the twenty-somethings I've spoken with are scared of even this minimal level of commitment. They think that by committing to an interest or field, they will be "closing the door" on their other interests and talents. If they were smart, they'd worry less about closing doors and more about getting a foot in one. It's tough to close a door that was never open to begin with.

Here are a few additional pieces of advice:

THERE'S NOTHING WRONG WITH A LITTLE FUSION, BUT AVOID "JAM BAND SYNDROME."

Musical artists often combine genres (i.e., "folk/rock" or "hip-hop/R&B") to create a unique sound for themselves. Similarly, you should feel free to fuse together a couple talents and interests in order to create a unique professional identity for yourself. You don't need to focus exclusively on one skill, nor should you limit your search to one industry. However, if you start cooking with too many ingredients, you run the risk of becoming the human equivalent of a "jam band." The vast majority of jam bands never get signed because they can't be counted on to produce a consistent product. Their songs sound different every time they are played, their solos often drown out melodies, and sometimes band members get too baked to function.* Why would Sony Music want to

---

*It's also worth noting that crappy jam bands are often paid in drugs and/or grilled cheese. If that sounds like the ideal compensation plan for you, you're probably reading the wrong book.

invest in that? They wouldn't. Similarly, why would anyone rush to hire a person whose résumé objective reads something like: "artistically inclined, analytically minded modern dancer hoping to pursue a career in day trading or construction"? They wouldn't.

SOLIDIFYING YOUR IDENTITY NOW ALLOWS YOU TO DIVERSIFY LATER.

Back in 1999, Metallica, one of the loudest, toughest, fastest, badass rock bands in the history of music, recorded an album with the San Francisco Symphony. The collaboration promptly went platinum. At first glance, it would seem as though the success of this experimental album completely undermines my hypothesis for this chapter, which is predicated on the need to commit to one sound. However, the reason fans and the industry cut Metallica some slack was because the band had, over the course of its career, developed an ironclad reputation as a loud, tough, fast, badass rock band.

By 1999 Metallica had *earned* the right to experiment a little bit because its track record was so strong. Fans trusted the band's ability to entertain, and the labels trusted the band's ability to sell albums. Similarly, fans and labels trusted Ray Charles when he recorded a country album in 1962, and gave Outkast the benefit of the doubt when it put together an experimental double album in 2003.

Once you make a name for yourself in your profession of choice, you will be granted a lot more leeway for experimentation and diversification. When it comes to landing your first deal (read: job) on the other hand, it is essential that you focus on producing a tight sound. Pick and stick with one angle, one brand, and start building buzz and a loyal fan base. That way, when you decide to branch out later on, you'll have an audience waiting to listen.

Desperate Housewives and the Era of Free Agency

IT USUALLY TAKES TIME TO LAND A STAR-MAKING ROLE.

BEFORE THE WOMEN of ABC's hit show *Desperate House-wives* became überfamous by backstabbing, eavesdropping, and sleeping their way around suburbia, they were merely five second-tier celebrities, jumping from role to role in search of an elevator to the A-list. Lost in the maze of Hollywood mediocrity and craving money, experience, and exposure, they pursued parts in a variety of genres, each hoping to land a star-making role. Between them, the Fab Five of *Desperate Housewives* took on roughly 160 different roles before landing on Wysteria Lane. That averages out to thirty-two jobs per housewife.

While I doubt that you will hold thirty-two different positions during the course of your career, you should expect to change roles at least a handful of times before you retire to a life of shuffleboard and 4:45 p.m. dinners at the Cracker Barrel. Most likely, the bulk of those moves will happen early on in your career. In today's fluid employment market, it can take a while before you land a star-making role. Therefore you shouldn't expect that your earliest gigs will be dream jobs. However, if you stay focused, work hard, and develop your strengths, you can position yourself to take advantage of the star-making opportunities.

There are countless reasons that you may leave a job—or it may leave you—and most of the time it has nothing to do with how talented you are. This chapter will highlight several of those reasons by focusing on early career moves made by the cast of *Desperate Housewives*.

GREAT CONCEPT, NO LEGS

Sometimes great ideas just don't catch on with the general public. All the talent in the world won't save your job if the masses don't dig what your company is trying to sell. Such was the case for Felicity Huffman ("Lynette" on *DHW*) with *Sports Night* in the late '90s. Critics loved Felicity as Dana Whitaker, the quick-witted and outspoken producer on the ESPN-esque satire. Additionally, the rest of the cast was talented, the writing was sharp, and Aaron Sorkin, the "can't miss" creator of *The West Wing*, was quarterbacking the whole thing. Sounds like a slam dunk, right? Eh . . . not so much. The snappy dialogue and "walk-and-talk" scenes that carried *West Wing* just didn't play as well with sitcom audiences. During the show's second season, ABC routinely pulled *Sports Night* in favor of bonus episodes of *Who Wants to Be a Millionaire* before canceling the show altogether.

GREAT ROLE, POOR TIMING

One could make the argument that Marcia Cross ("Bree") found her dramatic, sexy, backstabbing sweet spot long before she hit the mainstream on *Desperate Housewives*. In 1997 she portrayed Dr. Kimberly Shaw Mancini, a jealous and conniving spouse on Fox's

Melrose Place. For those of you who never saw the show, *Melrose* plotlines were eerily similar to those of *Desperate Housewives*–lots of sex, suspense, plot twists, and slapping. Unfortunately, Marcia joined the cast of *Melrose Place* when the show was way past its prime. By the time Dr. Kimberly Shaw Mancini detonated the military-strength explosives she had built in the basement, viewers had long since abandoned *Melrose* in favor of hot new shows like *Buffy the Vampire Slayer.* So, while Marcia's character blew up after roughly eight episodes, her career didn't blow up for another eight years.

If the company you work for runs into trouble or their products go out of style, not even an Emmy-winning performance on your part will lead to longevity. I mean, there were a lot of talented people working on the Sega Genesis marketing team in 1994, but they were doomed to fail because their product was being replaced in the market by Sony's hot new PlayStation. If you happen to join up with an organization that fails to catch fire or is already past its prime, don't get discouraged. Do your best and learn from the role while you have it.

YOU'VE BEEN MISCAST.

If you are young, talented, and ambitious, it is likely that you will be "fairly successful" in almost any professional role. Then again, who wants to settle for "fairly successful"? In 1989 Teri Hatcher ("Susan") got her first big-budget movie role portraying Sylvester Stallone's sweet yet spicy sister, Kiki Tango, in the buddy-cop action flick *Tango and Cash.* Though Teri did an admirable job and even created some sparks as Kurt Russell's love interest, her performance was nowhere near Oscar-worthy. Now I'm sure Teri could have crafted a "fairly successful" career in big-budget action films had she committed herself to doing so, but luckily she didn't settle. Instead she focused on snappier TV roles that showcased her sense of humor and eventually led her to *Desperate Housewives.** More than fifteen years later, *Tango and Cash* remains the lone big-budget action movie on Teri's résumé.

Don't settle for a career you might be fairly good at. Play to your strengths and pursue the roles in which you have a shot at being outstanding.

THE GIG WASN'T ALL IT WAS CRACKED UP TO BE.

In 2003, just three years after making her small-screen debut as "Flight Attendant #3" on *90210*, Eva Longoria ("Gabrielle") was poised to become a breakout star in Hollywood. In addition to the increasingly large roles she was receiving in movies, Eva had starred in multiple soap operas and also been named one of *People* magazine's "50 Most Beautiful People" (Spanish edition). Given her momentum at the time, it is somewhat surprising that her agents, managers, etc., allowed her to take on the role of "Carlita," a Miami nightclub performer trying to outrun the drug-dealing skeletons in her closet in the appropriately titled B-movie *Carlita's Secret*. Can you say "straight to DVD"? Obviously, some executive at the Maverick Entertainment Group gave Eva the pitch of a lifetime and convinced her that *Carlita* would make her the next Jennifer Lopez.

Like producers in Hollywood, executives in the corporate world will often oversell a position or their organization in an attempt to attract top talent. To be fair, I am in no position to criti-

---

*Terri's first star-making role came in the mid-'90s as Lois Lane on *Lois and Clark*. The show was the ideal transition between *Tango and Cash* and *Desperate Housewives*. It was action-oriented in spirit, but silly in its execution.

cize Eva's *Carlita* stint, given that I once accepted a job on the notion that I could somehow make up to 250K per year by analyzing shopping center parking lots for small-scale development. What can I say? The CEO made a great pitch and I didn't know enough about retail leasing and development to understand how difficult the job would actually be, or how long it would take to close enough deals to reach my goals. These days I do a lot more advance research before I accept a role.

YOU TOOK THE JOB BECAUSE YOU NEEDED THE MONEY.

Why else would Nicollette Sheridan ("Edie") sign on to do *Beverly Hills Ninja*? Financial strain forces millions of people to settle for suboptimal roles. If and when that happens in your career, make the best of the job until you are able to put yourself in a position to make a move to a more fulfilling role. Work hard, save your money, and keep your eyes open.

Your first job doesn't need to be perfect, and you should expect to switch organizations multiple times before you land your dream role. But in the meantime, you've got bills to pay. So if you find yourself working in the corporate equivalent of *Beverly Hills Ninja*, do your best to make the role work for you, and focus on developing skills that will help you capitalize when a better opportunity comes along.

PART TWO

Discovery Channels

GET YOUR HOMEWORK DONE BEFORE YOU GET
YOUR HUSTLE ON. IT'S HARD TO GET YOUR FOOT
IN THE DOOR WHEN IT'S ALREADY STUCK IN
YOUR MOUTH.

Give Yourself a Chance to Advance to Boardwalk

WHEN IT COMES TO "CHANCE ENCOUNTERS," YOU CAN'T GET LUCKY UNLESS YOU ROLL THE DICE.

STARTING A CONVERSATION on an airplane is like picking up a "Chance card" when playing Monopoly. Most Chance cards are not game-changing—maybe you have to pay a nominal poor tax of $15, or you net $10 by finishing second in a beauty contest. Worst-case scenario, you are sent off to jail for a three-roll stint or forced to kick some property taxes into the community. Nine times out of ten, "Chance" penalties are merely a minor annoyance.

On the other hand, the best Chance cards can immediately change the game. One minute you're earning your primary income from utilities or the low-rent district (Baltic/Mediterranean) and then all of a sudden you land on Chance and BAM! Boardwalk drops in your lap. Like Chance cards, "chance encounters" on airplanes, in the subway, in bars/restaurants, etc., can lead to game-changing career opportunities. Here's an example.

While flying from San Jose to Minneapolis during the spring of 1999, I had a chance encounter with a guy I will refer to as "Phil."

As it turned out, Phil worked in marketing for a little start-up company called "TiVo," which was designing a product that would allow people to record and fast-forward through live television (sound familiar?). Anyhow, we chatted for a couple of hours, both about his company and about my experiences in college, and in doing so we stumbled upon several points of shared interest. To make a long story short, by the time the captain put the seat belt sign on to signal our descent, Phil had offered me a summer internship with TiVo. (Unfortunately, I declined because I had already committed to working as a summer camp song leader. D'oh! On the bright side, I can now play a rockin' acoustic version of "This Land Is Your Land.")

When I tell the TiVo story to friends, the most common response (after they taunt me for not taking the job) is "Dude, I can't believe you just bumped into that guy." Guess what? It wasn't all dumb luck. Obviously I had no idea that I was going to sit next to the TiVo guy, but I did arrive at the airport two hours early in order to get a good seat, and I was the one who initiated our conversation. If you prepare yourself to stumble upon a golden opportunity, you probably won't end up stumbling at all.

CREATING "CHANCE ENCOUNTERS"

"Chance encounters" are often thought of as "unexpected," "casual," or "random." Why, then, do some people seem to get so much more out of them than others? It's simple really. They are better prepared. As a result, they have a better shot at turning their "chance" encounters into "successful" encounters.

For starters, successful people position themselves in spots where chance meetings are more likely to occur. Confucius say:

*She who wishes to encounter hotshots should frequent hot spots.** In other words, envision the type of people you would like to encounter "by chance" and then plant yourself in their habitat. For example, I sit in the exit row of airplanes whenever possible. More often than not, the exit row is populated by savvy business travelers who fly frequently and take advantage of the extra legroom. I've met several interesting businessmen and -women in the exit row, including the TiVo guy. Want to meet some stockbrokers? Spend some time at bars near your city's Financial District. Care to pick the brain of a police officer? Put in some Q.T. at Dunkin' Donuts. If you sit there they will come.

Keep in mind, many of the chats you initiate won't go anywhere and you're likely to get dragged into your fair share of awful conversations concerning pets, politics, or Sudoku. But that's a risk you've got to be willing to take. Remember, you only need to draw Boardwalk once to change the outcome of the game.

---

*I'm totally lying. Confucius never said that. I doubt you really care.

Google and Schmooze

IN THE TWENTY-FIRST CENTURY, NETWORKING IS USELESS WITHOUT THE "NET."

THREE YEARS AGO I made a fool of myself in Kansas City. It happened while I was attending a preconvention cocktail party. Given the casual air and liberal allotment of drink tickets, I knew the gathering would provide ample opportunity for networking. My goal was to target top executives who had blown off my earlier attempts at contact, engage them in casual conversation by the bar or shrimp tray, and then convince them to meet with me the following day on the convention floor. I knew it would be nearly impossible to get impromptu face time with shot-calling execs the next day, unless I was willing to linger near the Starbucks cart all morning and wait for head honchos to mosey on by for a half-caf vanilla latte. I may be ambitious but I'm not "that guy."

Anyhow, the cocktail party in question was being held on the top floor of a swanky office building. Shortly after arriving, I set my sights on a man in a bright pink suit, roughly midfifties. I figured (correctly) that any man with the stones to wear a flamingo coat to a business function must be extremely confident in himself and, more important, his standing in the room. His nametag confirmed my suspicions:

R.J. Mulligan*
President, R.J. Mulligan Companies, Inc.

I positioned myself beside Mr. Mulligan in the appetizer line and took my shot. Picking up a pair of tongs, I poked around curiously in one of the buffet bins.

"Pork taquitos, eh? I just don't think I have the courage tonight," I said to nobody in particular (though Mulligan and I were the only two in line). Mulligan took the bait.

"Wise move, my friend. Live to fight another day."

"I think I will," I replied. "After all, I've gotta go out and buy myself a pastel tuxedo tomorrow."

Mulligan beamed. "You like?" he asked, opening the coat to reveal equally tacky pink suspenders. I was in.

"Very elegant," I chuckled.

Mulligan asked me where my company was based, and when I answered "Denver," he went off about how he had just returned from a ski weekend in Vail. I smiled and asked "how the powder was," as though I had a frame of reference for ski conditions (I did not).

"Insane, man" was his reply.

Note: When you are talking with an older person and he/she forces contemporary slang into the conversation, that's a very good sign. It means that he/she views you as the "cooler" vs. simply the "younger" party. That is a major status distinction.

Five minutes and three R.J. Mulligan ski adventure tales later, I decided to steer the conversation back to business, hoping to un-

---

*Not his real name.

cover some commonalities that would necessitate the scheduling of a meeting the next day at the convention.

"So, R.J., how's business?" I asked. "I mean, what keeps you guys busy at the R.J. Mulligan Companies these days?"

The smile faded from Mulligan's face and was instantly replaced by a look of disdain. While he did start to tell me about his company's specialty, he also began looking over, above, and around me as he spoke. When I tried to explain how there might be some synergies between his company and my own, he just nodded mechanically, said, "Good luck with that," and proceeded to overtly blow me off. Two seconds later he "spotted" an acquaintance he had supposedly been meaning to talk to for months and shuffled off, leaving me a little stunned.

At first I didn't understand what I had done wrong, but it didn't take me long to figure it out.* Looking around, I noticed several people in the room were wearing "R.J. Mulligan Companies, Inc." nametags, and then there was the banner advertising R.J. Mulligan as a major sponsor of the event. Shit. For all intents and purposes R.J. Mulligan was the emcee of the evening and I didn't know who he was or what his company did. As one of the most sought after conversations in the room, R.J. had no reason to waste time explaining the basics of his business to me. What a rookie move! Had I spent five minutes on the Internet before the event I could've easily Googled the guy and his company and avoided the whole mishap.

The moral here is that you should always do your homework on the Net before heading off to networking events. Find out who the sponsors are, figure out who's going to be attending, then take a few minutes to thoroughly Google them all. A little background check goes a long way toward impressing somebody you happen to bump into in the taquito line.

---

*For starters, I had used the word "synergy."

Swallow Your "Phone Pride"

IF AT FIRST THEY DON'T PICK UP, TRY, TRY AGAIN.

"**PHONE PRIDE**" **IS** for losers. When your career is involved, you can't afford to wait your turn. It doesn't matter whether you are trying to reach a potential employer, investors, a colleague, or a peer who has information you need. If the person you're pursuing doesn't return your first call, you shouldn't assume you are being screened. He or she is probably just busy. Making a second attempt at communication does not make you pathetic or Toolish; it makes you persistent and proactive. On the other hand, eight or nine unanswered calls in a row makes you a stalker.

Here are a few tips to help you find a happy medium:

DIVERSIFY YOUR COMMUNICATION CHANNELS.

Being persistent doesn't have to mean being awkwardly repetitive. Diversifying your communication channels will give you the best chance to reach your target. Ever seen the '80s classic *Say Anything*? In the film, Lloyd Dobler (John Cusack) falls head over heels for the foxy high school valedictorian, Diane Court. Unfortunately for Lloyd, Diane stops returning his phone calls about eighty minutes into the movie. Does Lloyd give up? Hell no! But does he keep calling and leaving one pathetic message after another like Jon Favrau in *Swingers*? Hell no!

Lloyd realizes that Diane might be more responsive to other communication channels, so he puts down the phone, picks up a boom box, and plants himself outside her window (in the rain). Lo and behold, the switch works and Lloyd and Diane live happily ever after.

Note: I am not advocating that you go plant yourself outside your boss's office and blast a Peter Gabriel cassette. Remember, Say Anything *was made in the '80s. That means there were no Treos, pagers, or even the Internet, for Pete's sake. It's not like Lloyd could just shoot Diane an IM. Luckily, as a citizen of the twenty-first century, you've got lots of options. With so many devices at your fingertips, you can mask your impatience by using multiple mediums. Instead of peppering an unresponsive party with the same awkward voice mails every week, send an e-mail or shoot him or her an instant message.**

MIX UP YOUR MESSAGES.

Mixing up your content is crucial when making multiple attempts to get in touch with someone. Sure, the central directive of "please get back to me when you get a moment" should stay consistent, but you should put some thought into varying your messages so that you don't sound like a broken record. For instance, consider the following three examples:

---

*Note: Instant messages should be used only in instances when you have an established personal relationship with the contact in question.

- "Derek, it's Jenny calling. I really enjoyed our conversation last month. I know you must be swamped, but I'd love to grab lunch once you get your head above water.

- "Derek, I saw that your CEO decided to step down. Any indication of who the replacement might be? Drop me a line when you get a moment."

- "Derek, USC 33, Florida 14? I guess this means it's time for the Gators to start recruiting out of state. Let's discuss over coffee this week."

All three examples have the same core message (get back to me) but each contains a secondary, personalized reason for reaching out.

SPACE OUT AND CHILL OUT.

Put a little space between your solicitations. That way, your targets will know that you are eager to get ahold of them, but you won't come off as desperate or creepy. You don't want to be the Tool who sends eight messages in the same day. Actually, you don't want to be the Tool who sends eight messages, period. Three or four attempts to contact someone is more than adequate.

Also, if you encounter a target at random during the day, don't put him or her on the spot with an "I sent you two e-mails, why haven't you gotten back to me?" confrontation. Play it cool.

BE READY TO RECEIVE.

In *One Crazy Summer*, a lesser-known Cusack classic from the '80s,* "Uncle Frank" spends all summer glued to the phone, dialing and chain-smoking, trying to get through to a radio station in hopes of winning their million-dollar call-in contest. Near the end of the movie, Uncle Frank finally gets through to the DJ but he gets so excited that he pulls the phone cord out of the wall, disconnects the call, and gets disqualified. One of the last scenes of the movie shows Frank firing a missile at the radio station.

Persistence won't do you any good if you aren't prepared when your contact calls back. Check your e-mail regularly and keep any notes or information pertinent to the conversation on hand. Oh yeah, also make sure you charge your phone and pay your bills. The last thing you need is for your target to hear a *This number has been temporarily disconnected* message because you forgot to mail a check to T-Mobile.

---

*Costarring Demi Moore.

A Fellowship of Nine to Guide You

ASSEMBLE AN INFORMAL CREW OF "ADVISORS" TO DIRECT YOUR CAREER.

ALMOST ALL GREAT cinematic "quests" involve a band of diverse characters who, despite being thrown together by circumstances beyond their control, must overcome many obstacles to persevere in a hostile world. It doesn't matter whether the end goal of the quest is to save the world (à la *Lord of the Rings*), score some treasure (*The Goonies*), gain a sense of self (*The Breakfast Club*), or capture superficial celebrity status (*Spice World*), a well-rounded team is a requirement for success. As the journey progresses, it becomes clear that each character in the group possesses unique talents and assets that come in handy along the way–think Legolas's keen eyesight (*LOTR*), Data's "Pinchers of Power" (*Goonies*), or Claire's ability to apply lipstick with her cleavage (*Breakfast Club*). Your career is no different. You may be the hero in the story, but you need a solid crew to back you up, lest you lose your way, reach an impasse, or fall victim to bloodthirsty Orcs and angry Frattellis.

Whether you need inside tips on job opportunities or openings, interview advice, or simply someone to kick around ideas with, setting up a personal team of trusted career advisors will prove priceless. Don't fool yourself into thinking that you need to venture into the dangerous wilderness by yourself like Leonidas in *300* in order to prove your worth. Your friends, your parents' friends, friends of friends, former bosses, professors, coworkers, and random peers you admire could all be candidates for your crew. Whomever you select, it is important that you keep in mind the following points.

FORM FRIENDSHIPS FIRST.

I've seen several publications refer to one's personal network as a "personal board of directors." That's a terrible and Toolish idea if you ask me. The focus of a board of directors is to discuss one subject only—the success of a single organization, entity, brand, and so forth. Your goal should be to develop relationships that extend beyond the specifics of your career. You need to form friendships first if you want true support on your quest. I mean, would Frodo Baggins have been able to destroy the ring if not for the selfless devotion of true friends and mentors? How would Ginger Spice have been able to withstand the perils of overexposure and the paparazzi if not for the emotional support and choreography of Sporty and Scary? Sure, relationships that are strictly business can be useful, but genuine friends are the ones who will help you get what you want, what you really really want.

MAKE TIME FOR EACH MEMBER.

You should aim to contact every one of your informal advisors on a regular basis, say every three months or so. Don't settle for leaving a message or simply writing a quick e-mail, either. Get ahold of each individual on the phone or go see him or her in person. If you want to make well-rounded and informed decisions every time, you need to receive input and advice from multiple sources every time. That means you can't just stay close with one or two mentors and let the other relationships deteriorate.

WATCH OUT FOR SELLOUTS.

Quest movies also teach us to beware of the "trusted" advisor with ulterior motives. Granted, I doubt any of the people in your network will have the diabolical intent of Verbal Kint from *The Usual Suspects*, Sir Leigh Teabing from *The Da Vinci Code*, or Gríma Wormtongue from *Lord of the Rings: The Two Towers* (by the way, how did the king not see that coming? The guy's last name was "Wormtongue" for the love!). However, it is possible that self-interest might drive somebody in your crew to pass along poor advice. For that reason (and others), external advice should be processed in conjunction with the research you do on your own. If you get lazy and accept advice as fact, no matter the source, you will leave yourself susceptible to manipulation.

Party On, Wayne

SOCIAL GATHERINGS CAN BE GREAT FOR EXPANDING YOUR BUSINESS NETWORK, AS LONG AS YOU UNDERSTAND THE RULES OF ENGAGEMENT.

THE FOLLOWING IS a true story. I swear I'm not making this up. I've got witnesses.

During the spring of 2001 I was awarded a couple thousand bucks in grant money to do a summer research project in Japan. After purchasing my plane ticket and paying rent on my apartment in California for the time I'd be away, I was left with roughly $1,000 for a month's worth of food, lodging, and all other expenses in Tokyo. Tokyo is one of the most (if not *the* most) expensive cities in the world, so I was resigned to the fact that I was probably going to end up spending August crashing on a tatami mat in a train station bathroom, 40 kilometers outside of the city center. The daily transportation costs alone threatened to limit the number of face-to-face meetings I would be able to schedule for my project. That is, until the following events took place at a July 4 party in Los Angeles, circa 2 a.m. *(Cue Wayne and Garth's flashback/daydream noises: "Doodle-a-doo doodle-a-doo.")*

I had to get some air. My legs were tired from dancing and my ears were ringing thanks to my buddy Brad, who had been blasting O.A.R.'s "Crazy Game of Poker" on repeat for a full hour. While scanning the backyard for a chair on which to pass out, I stumbled upon a random guy who was sizing up the pool as a possible receptacle for some post-keg relief.

"Whoa! Man, that's probably not a good idea." I am not always the whistle-blower at parties, but in this case the host was a good friend.

"But I gotta go," he said with the sincerity of a kindergartner.

"Okay. All I'm saying is you should turn toward the lawn."

"Sure, sure, sure." Down went his zipper.

"Seriously, dude . . . you really don't want to take a leak in the pool. Not here."

"Kids do it all the time."

"Right, when they are IN the pool . . . and kids."

"Riiiiight." Something clicked upstairs and he turned toward the lawn. (Thirty seconds of fertilization later.) "Thanks, man. I'm really out of it right now. I flew in from Tokyo this morning."

"Really? I'm going there next month."

"Cool. Where are you staying?"

"Not sure. I'm still weighing my options" (like I had options).

"Dude, you should crash at my place. My roommate just took a job in New York and I've got an extra bedroom."

"No shit?" I am not an articulate drunk. "Let me grab your e-mail address before you take off."

As it turned out, the Pool Pisser was a laid-back finance guy with an epic apartment in the middle of Tokyo. So instead of crashing in a train station bathroom, I spent August in a pad with a temperature-controlled spa tub (for free). Not only was I able to complete all of my planned research activities, but I also had a little extra money to cause trouble during my downtime. And to think that I almost didn't go to the party . . .

The point of this story is not to highlight the benefits of being the pool police, but rather to point out that parties, cookouts, bars, and other social events are all great places to make professional contacts, as long as you abide by a few simple rules of engagement for social gatherings. Should you elect to disregard said rules by treating social gatherings like professional events, you run the serious risk of coming off like a Corporate Tool, alienating your friends, and never getting invited to anything ever again (except when nobody else feels like driving).

Before diving into the rules themselves, I'm going to provide a basic framework for differentiating between conduct that is suitable for a professional gathering and that which is appropriate in social environments. Check out the chart that follows:

VENUE	Professional Gathering	Social Gathering
Your purpose, first and foremost	To work	To chill
Slang usage	Professional slang is expected; social slang is a no-no (e.g., "I was sooo faded last night").	Social slang is expected; professional slang is a no-no (e.g., "Tonight is great for my work/life balance").
Small talk	Keep social conversations short and sweet. You weren't hired to be a gossip.	Keep professional conversations short and sweet. You weren't invited to be a douche bag.
Digit discretion	Don't give out your home phone number while seated at a crowded conference table.	Don't pass out business cards at a crowded dinner table.
If you want to see what happens when you ignore the rules, check this out	Demi Moore in *Disclosure* (1994)	Campbell Scott in *The Spanish Prisoner* (1997)

On to the rules.

PICK YOUR OPPORTUNITIES.

Not every opportunity is an appropriate opportunity. In the opening scene of the movie *Cadillac Man*, Robin Williams's character happens upon a funeral procession stalled on the side of the road (the hearse broke down). Williams, being the shady salesman that he is, offers the widow his condolences then quickly offers her a rate on a new car. Her response: "You're not trying to sell me a car, are you? At my husband's funeral? Before he's even in the ground? Are you? You sleaze! You are the scum of the earth."

In nonprofessional settings, you need to exercise discretion before talking shop. If you bump into a potential business partner or find yourself chatting with an ideal investor, take a second to survey the scene before bringing up work. Some social settings are simply off-limits. An astounding number of Corporate Tools simply can't grasp this concept, which is why, again, they are not usually invited out (unless nobody else feels like driving).

READ THE SUBTLE CUES.

So, what do you do? is just a polite question. It is NOT an invitation for a sales pitch, a recitation of your résumé, a description of your company's business units, or an hour-long narration on your daily responsibilities. On the other hand, if the question is followed by multiple specific follow-up questions about your professional life, the other party may actually be interested. Pay attention to facial expressions and body language. Hint: if they start dozing off, better steer the conversation away from your company's mission statement.

CONDUCT PSYCHO DUE DILIGENCE.

Ever seen *Sleeping with the Enemy*? No matter how cool someone seems in a social setting, it is always best to take it slow and make sure that he/she isn't a psycho stalker before you strike a deal or make concrete plans to join forces. Do you think I asked for the Pool Pisser's keys on the night we met at the party? Not a chance. We made arrangements over the course of several weeks and e-mails, when we were both at our desks, sober, and neither of us had his fly unzipped.

If you meet someone at a party with whom you'd like to do business, exchange cards or e-mail addresses, but save the actual deal making for later.

CH. 9

Technical Party Fouls

DON'T BLOW NETWORKING OPPORTUNITIES WITH
UNSPORTSMANLIKE CONDUCT.

URBANDICTIONARY.COM DEFINES A "party foul" as the following: *an action committed by an individual, either on purpose or not, that goes against the feel of the party*...As such, all of the following could be appropriately labeled "party fouls":

> *Pouring beer in the dog bowl.*
> *Slapping the host.*
> *Hurling on the couch.*
> *Double-dipping your tortilla chips (especially when you've got a cold).*

It goes without saying that any action that might constitute a party foul at a friend's birthday party would also be frowned upon at a professional event. You don't need me to tell you that it's a bad idea to grab a handful of artichoke dip from the buffet line, or make a pass at somebody's spouse. Nor do you need me to tell you that you are more likely to engage in said idiotic activities if you consume more beers than you have fingers (seven beers + office party + karaoke machine + "I Touch Myself" = a really awkward Monday). Therefore I'm not going to waste my energy rehashing the dangers of committing flagrant party fouls, even though it might be funny. Instead I would like to focus on the less obvious party fouls—the subtle infractions that won't get you arrested, banned from a venue, or fired, but will unquestionably draw negative attention and possibly do some lasting damage to your professional reputation.

I like to think of these fouls as "technical party fouls." For those of you who don't watch sports, a "technical foul" is awarded in basketball when a player commits an unsportsmanlike act. While technical fouls are occasionally awarded for things like inciting brawls or spitting on fans, most "Ts" (as they are called) are doled out for more minor outbursts, like shouting at an official or flipping one's headband into the stands.

The following are examples of technical party fouls to avoid at all costs during professional or work-related gatherings:

FAILING TO USE YOUR "INSIDE VOICE"

Corporate Tools can't seem to control the volume of their voices in social settings, particularly after they've knocked back a little bit of Grandpa's old cough medicine. Fact: The volume of your voice is not positively correlated to others' desire to hear what you have to say. There's really no need to broadcast your conversations through multiple rooms.

ASKING INAPPROPRIATE QUESTIONS

"Great outfit, Lisa. How much did that set you back?"
"Whoa, Phil, your girlfriend is smokin'! Are those real?"
"No, seriously, who do you think would win in a fight—me or
 O'Connell from auditing?"

Get a reputation for asking awkward questions like these and people around the office will start avoiding you like Hollywood avoids carbs.

EXCESSIVE COMPLAINING

Everyone likes to blow off steam every now and again by venting about their jerk of a boss, or how underappreciated they are by management, or how it's been two years since their last raise. This is perfectly normal, and even healthy. But whatever you do, *don't* do it at a crowded professional function. Your complaints will inevitably reach the wrong ears, and nothing good will come of it.

MOST Ts OCCUR WHILE PLAYERS ARE EMOTIONALLY CHARGED.

Don't let yourself get drawn into heated arguments while you're in a social atmosphere. It doesn't matter if you're talking about politics, the Red Sox, or who got kicked off *America's Next Top Model*; if you sense you are starting to get riled up, take a deep breath or excuse yourself from the conversation.

TWO Ts AND YOU'RE GONE.

From youth leagues to the NBA, the rule is universal. Two technical fouls in the same game and you will get tossed. Most social and professional events are the same way. Multiple outbursts will lead you straight to the door, and it's hard to make connections or create opportunities when you're sitting on the curb.

PART THREE

Pimp My Résumé

Bust Out the "Special Edition"

MARKETING YOURSELF LIKE A MOVIE WILL HELP
YOUR RÉSUMÉ FLY OFF THE SHELF.

WHEN SUBMITTING YOUR résumé to any professional organization, you should expect that the people on the receiving end will review it with roughly the same attention span and scrutiny as a seven-year-old checking out DVDs at Blockbuster. That means that you need to appear exciting and colorful, yet somewhat familiar, at first glance or you'll never get rented. Seven-year-olds don't care much for mysteries or suspense. They make their selections based on predictability and past experience, which is why they choose the same movies over and over and over again. Kids will take one quick look at a given box and if nothing on the cover screams "WOW! FUN! WOW!" they won't whine for their parents to reach up and grab it off the shelf. Instead they'll select *Shrek* for the five hundredth time or simply lose interest in movie rentals altogether.

Speaking as someone who has participated in the professional hiring process and been forced to sift through tons of résumés, I can assure you that HR (Human Resources) execs are the same way. Your résumé will get a quick once-over, and if nothing jumps

out and screams "QUALIFIED! UNIQUE! AN UNQUESTION-
ABLE ASSET," they won't whine to the department heads to
snatch you off the market. If you really want to fly off the unem-
ployment shelf, you need some kick-ass DVD packaging. Your résumé needs to do more than simply inform. It must demand the
attention of browsing HR managers and executives and shout,
"This is a must-meet person!" or "One of the top five candidates
of the year! Truly outstanding!"

Once your résumé attracts the elusive gaze of potential employers, it must follow through by providing concise answers to the
questions at the heart of the DVD selection process: Why should
I select this person? Will he or she make me laugh or cry? Will he
or she surprise me, make me think, or inspire me? At the very least,
will he or she keep me entertained?

Movie studios have spent billions of dollars addressing similar
questions and I think the lessons they have learned are easily applied to the world of employment. As such, I implore you to pay
close attention to the following "DVD résumé" tips:

GIVE 'EM THE GIST RIGHT AWAY.

You want to know why wordy movie summaries are positioned on
the back (as opposed to the front) of DVD cases? Because no one
gives a @#%$, that's why. At least not right away. Background
and synopsis mean nothing to me until I make the initial call between "heartwarming," "side-splittingly funny," or "full-throttle
entertainment." Do you hear what I'm saying? For example, go
check out the DVD cover for the 1998 teen comedy *Can't Hardly
Wait* (you can find it on imdb.com).

Within ten seconds of viewing the *Can't Hardly* cover, anyone
can see that this is a coming-of-age flick about high school's last
hurrah. Immediately, we recognize that the cast contains the req-

uisite hot girl, obnoxious loudmouth, abused geek, and quirky kid with weird eyewear. Just like that, we've gotten the gist of the movie. We've been sufficiently pitched, but not alienated by unrequested detail. Now, if it turns out that we're in the mood for a late '90s comedy with an ensemble cast of attractive twentysomethings portraying high school caricatures, we'll know enough to grab this movie (along with *Varsity Blues* and *She's All That*) off the shelf and dive into the details before making a final selection.

Though I'm sure you can hardly wait to tell potential employers every impressive detail about your worldly experience and winning attributes, make sure that your audience doesn't need to look too far to get the gist. Position your strongest experiences near the top of the page. Also, state your work and educational experiences concisely and quantitatively. Focus on what you've accomplished as opposed to vague statements or titles that don't mean anything. For example, if you spent time working as a software engineer, list the programs you worked on, your role on the team, and the results of the team's work. If you created something individually, throw that in there as well. Use bullets for your details. Your résumé is not a forum for describing your journeys. There will be plenty of time for that later on during interviews.

AVOID "OBJECTIVES."

I object to objectives. When it comes to the résumés of relatively inexperienced and vaguely ambitious young professionals (see: you), "Objectives" sections are not usually productive. What good is stating your employment expectations and hopes if you have no idea what you want? I recently had a conversation with my friend Angela about this. Angela is a senior HR executive at a major bank. She has sifted through thousands of résumés in her career and she can't recall a single instance in which a young candidate's

"Objectives" section made a positive impact by revealing new qualifications that weren't already apparent in the résumé. As she says: "I don't lose anything when 'Objectives' are left out. If anything, 'Objectives' are more likely to have a negative effect." Angela then went on to recall several common "Objectives" pitfalls, like listing objectives for the wrong industry, or unrealistic objectives (example: "I would like to be CEO within five years") that reveal a candidate's overinflated sense of self-worth. "Sometimes it's tough to tell if they're really ambitious or just lunatics," Angela says. Bottom line: Ambitious "Objectives" don't make you any more qualified. Prior experiences and achievements say far more about your talent and ambition than flowery adjectives planted in a weak "Objective."

PUBLISH ONLY STRONG REVIEWS.

I've seen a lot of employment literature that suggests stating one's college GPA on the résumé is a must. What a load! My theory on GPAs is as follows: Earning a 4.0 in college is like earning a rave review from a critic. If you managed to achieve such a feat, you definitely want potential employers to know about it. On the other hand, you wouldn't want to advertise a two-star review, so why promote a mediocre GPA? If you didn't do so hot in class, focus on work experience and extracurriculars. Pick and choose. You don't have to put anything in your résumé that doesn't make you look good. If Ebert and Roeper didn't like you, go with Peter Travers from *Rolling Stone*.

HIGHLIGHT SPECIAL FEATURES.

If you've been to Blockbuster or shopped online for movies in the past five years, you are undoubtedly aware that every DVD possesses a host of special features such as deleted scenes, bloopers, and star commentary. These special features don't alter the core story of the film, but they can enhance the viewing experience. Same goes for your résumé. In addition to listing the features that package you as a qualified candidate, you also need to advertise the hobbies/activities/interests that make you "Uncut, Unrated, and Unbelievable." Do you play the fiddle or speak Portuguese? Have you mastered Dance Dance Revolution VII? The little quirks that round out your personality can and will help you rise to the top of the résumé pile. I mean, who wouldn't want to interview a yo-yo master or the California State Logrolling Champion?

CH. 11

Lose the Mad Libs

ALL COVER LETTERS SHOULD NOT BE CREATED EQUAL.

T HE VAST MAJORITY of cover letters are nothing more than longhand regurgitations of an applicant's résumé. They reek of uninteresting fill-in-the-blank formality, kind of like a Mad Lib with no jokes. Hey, Mad Libs are great for rainy days up at the lake or family car trips, but not for job applications. Yet most cover letters go something like this:

Dear _____, I am writing to apply for the
     Proper Noun

vacant _____ position. I believe that
     Organizational Role

_____ is an extremely _____
 Company Name   Adjective

_____, and I would love the _____ to con-
 Noun   Noun

tinue my career in such a _____ envi-
                Suck-up Adjective

ronment, which I feel matches perfectly with my

_____ talents and _____ .
Unnecessary Adjective   Plural Noun

Painful, isn't it? Now imagine being an HR director who is forced to read several hundred of these a week. Mad Lib cover letters are generic and uninspiring. Nothing about them looks heartfelt or well thought out, and most employers can spot them from a mile away. I'm not saying that every aspect of your cover letter needs to be 100 percent unique. However, you should take the time to individualize each letter beyond the Mad Lib level.

Good cover letters are like good love songs, because they show your target that not only do you want to "get with" them but you also "get" them, meaning you understand what they're all about—their business, their identity, and their vision. On the other hand, bad cover letters, like bad love songs, fail to convey genuine attraction. Thus audiences are left apathetic and annoyed. For example, consider the following stanza, taken from LFO's awful 1999 love jam, "Summer Girls."*

You're the best girl that I ever did see
The great Larry Bird Jersey 33

Whoever wrote this ditty obviously thought that if he just said "you're the best," he could follow it up with whatever the hell he wanted and still get lucky. I mean, the next line is totally unrelated. Larry Bird? That's absurd, right? Of course it is, yet millions of job applicants put the same type of generic non sequiturs in their cover letters. For example,

---

*LFO stood for "Lyte Funky Ones." If you recall, they liked girls who wore Abercrombie and Fitch.

Your company is really exciting. I am a really passionate person and a hard worker.

That is just as hokey and unconvincing as LFO (without the frosted tips). If you can't prove that you "get" a given organization, or even explain why you want to "get with" them, you shouldn't waste your time. The cover letter is your first opportunity to prove that you are serious about landing a given job; that you've researched the company's products and services, kept up with their recent deals, and, most important, that you can communicate exactly why you've chosen *them* over all the other fish in the sea.

Focus on the fit between you and the target organization. What skills do you possess that are tailor-made for their organization, specifically? Don't just list what you're good at. They'll get that in your résumé. Instead, take the Jerry McGuire approach. Organizations will be more likely to show you the money if you can clearly explain the ways in which you will "complete them."*

---

*I apologize for referencing the "you complete me" line. But come on, it's so cheap and cheesy that it will be nearly impossible to forget.

PART FOUR

Nailing the Audition

INTERVIEW INSIGHTS AND TIPS FOR STAYING
COOL ON THE HOT SEAT

The Rules of Interview Dating

TIPS TO HELP YOU SCORE . . . A JOB

NTERVIEWING IS A lot like dating. After all, both pursuits involve varying levels of anticipation, conversation, humiliation, and (if you get lucky) consummation. It makes sense, therefore, that many of the skills and mentalities that help you score in the dating world should also work in the interview world. Here are some tips to help you get ~~action~~ hired:

NEVER TURN DOWN A DRINK.

Take as many interviews as possible, even if you don't necessarily want to work for the company pursuing you. The more interviews you attend the more confident and polished you will become. Don't worry about developing a reputation as a "job tease." Accepting an interview merely suggests that you will engage another party in conversation. It doesn't mean you have to take the job any more than accepting a drink means you are committing to a relationship. In both cases, you owe it to yourself to learn what's out there. It will be tough to stay focused on any new gig if a part of you always wonders if the grass might be greener somewhere else.

YOU DON'T HAVE TO MARRY THE FIRST PERSON WHO TRIES TO KISS YOU (UNLESS HE OR SHE IS ALL THAT).

In college and grad school hard work is rewarded with good grades, academic honors, and eventually (one hopes) a degree. Unfortunately, a degree by itself won't provide you with the means to buy a second pair of jeans, rent an apartment with air-conditioning, or remove the duct tape holding in the window of your seventeen-year-old hatchback. It is understandable, therefore, that a high percentage of recent grads eagerly sign their life over to the first company that offers them some cash. To these eager beavers, I offer the following word of caution: "You don't have to marry the first person who tries to kiss you." I know, once the offer has been put on the table it's hard to look away, especially when you're desperate. And sometimes the first job can end up being Mr. (or Ms.) Right. Still, try to exhibit some restraint and play it cool. Again, you shouldn't commit until you have a good idea of what's out there.

WHY FOCUS ON YOUR EX?

Everyone has had relationships that didn't work out in the past. It's important to be honest about why you're back on the market, but don't smother your date (interviewer) with stories about everything that went wrong with your ex (last job). You don't want to come off as bitter, or worse, "damaged goods."

Speaking of damaged goods, try not to volunteer any personal or professional flaws during interviews. There's nothing wrong with addressing areas you'd like to improve, but don't be too candid about your professional or personal shortcomings. Nothing kills a spark like the following: "To be honest, I didn't know how I'd ever be able to get close to a job ever again. Luckily, my new meds do a good job at keeping my, um, 'issues' from flaring up."

Don't go there.

Assume Your Positioning

WHAT SETS YOU APART FROM ALL THE OTHER PRODUCTS IN THE STORE?

MY YOUNGER BROTHER, David, was hired as a Navy SEAL commander when he was only twenty-two years old. Though he had no prior military background or weapons training, David was still deemed the right man for the job. When he called and told me he had landed the gig, I was incredibly proud but really surprised. Who would have thought that my little brother would ever become a high-ranking military officer? Not me. He must have made a great impression in his interview.

The coolest part of the whole thing was that less than six months later I was able to watch David lead his men through hostile territory and scramble down a hill covered in fiery shrapnel. It was the best (and only) episode of *JAG* I ever watched.

First-round job interviews are often conducted in much the same manner as TV guest-star auditions. In early guest-star auditions, casting directors (CDs) will scan your résumé, ask you to say a few things, and decide then and there whether you fit the profile. The whole process takes roughly five to fifteen minutes. CDs have a specific role to fill, a budget for that role, and a pretty good idea of the type of person they're looking for. If the CDs like you, you'll get called back for a screen test. If not, you'll never hear from them again. The whole experience is somewhat superficial and extremely subjective but, hey, that's life.

Early-round job interviews aren't much different. You sit down across the table from someone who scans your résumé (often for the first time) and then waits to hear what you have to say. More often than not, he or she will make a judgment about whether or not you are right for the role after less than twenty minutes of face time. Then he or she will either punch your ticket to the next round or send you packing.

Given that early interviews afford you so little time to perform, it is absolutely essential that you make a great first impression. Here are three ways you can prepare to nail the audition:

RESEARCH THE ROLE.

My older sister, Cara, is also a professional actress (what happened to me, right?). When Cara has an audition coming up, she sometimes spends up to eight hours researching the role. By the time she walks into the space where the audition is being held, she knows everything about the character—her likes and dislikes, her background, her relationships, and her motivations—backward and forward. I suggest you do the same in advance of your interviews. Hit the books (see: Internet) and learn the role you are pursuing inside and out. How will you interact with the other characters in the organization? What will you be called upon to do when drama unfolds? Most important, what traits do you have that will both elevate and differentiate your performance from that of other candidates?

POSITION YOURSELF.

In the marketing world, "positioning" refers to the distinctive and identifying qualities and characteristics that draw consumers to your product rather than someone else's. For example, Subway's positioning is "Fresh and Healthy," while KFC aims for "Hearty and Homecooked." Personal positioning isn't much different from product positioning. When done well, it will plant your distinct professional image in the minds of your target audience.

When my friend Dave Flemming interviewed for a spot on the San Francisco Giants' radio broadcast team in 2003, he wanted to make sure that the Giants had a very clear idea of who he was and what he stood for. As he put it:

> "If I was selling myself to any of these people who were hiring me, I tried to sell myself as someone who was thoughtful, had some smarts, but was not coming in to be a star and get rich. I told them that I wasn't going to try to be a know-it-all. I had respect for the fans and their intelligence."

Unlike many of his competitors who tried to use on-air opportunities to showcase their range as entertainers and impress the Giants with witty commentary and wacky catchphrases (like "Whammy!" à la Champ, the sportscaster from the movie *Anchorman*), Dave made a point to reinforce the fact that he believed his job was to keep the fans informed, rather than simply to make them laugh. The ball club agreed and Dave has been a fixture on San Francisco Giants' broadcasts ever since.

MAKE A TEN-SECOND COMMERCIAL.

If you are having trouble shaping your personal positioning, I suggest developing a "commercial" to use whenever you need to make a professional introduction. Sometimes called an "elevator pitch," the commercial should explain who you are and what makes you unique in no more than ten seconds. Keep in mind, your commercial should be much more low-key than a "break-dancing gecko" TV commercial. You don't need a catchy tagline, a sexy voice, or a jingle. Just put a couple of thoughts together expressing who you are, what you want to do, and why you would be great at it.

Ten seconds may not seem like a long time to you, but it is for your audience. When you consider that major ad agencies are given only thirty seconds (and occasionally break-dancing geckos) to convince millions of people that their quality of life will increase exponentially if they go out and buy low-carb beer, fruity shampoo, or wrinkle-free khakis, your task seems far less daunting.

When it comes to early interviews, first impressions are the only impressions. Be ready. Research the role you are auditioning for and fine-tune your personal positioning. Set yourself apart from the generic, bottom-shelf brands.

CH. 14

Schooled in Rock

LEARN WHAT'S HOT AND WHAT'S NOT BEFORE
YOU INTERVIEW.

"LEWIS"* IS A musician friend of mine in Nashville. Unlike most of my musician friends, Lewis actually makes his living playing music. In addition to gigs with his primary band, he does session work for other artists, records film sound tracks, and plays main stages at festivals across the country.

Though only in his twenties, Lewis has managed to build quite a reputation for himself in industry circles. Two years ago that reputation earned him an invitation to a very special audition. He and five other musicians were flown out to the East Coast to vie for the chance to play alongside a rock legend during a three-month European tour. Just so you know, I don't throw the term "legend" around lightly. This guy was a bona fide Hall of Famer. I'm not talking about Duncan Sheik or Lisa Loeb, comprende?

Anyhow, Lewis left the audition feeling great. He had played

---

*At the request of the principal subject, all names and locations have been changed. Musicians never trust writers.

well, vibed with the legend and his band, and had a great time. Unfortunately, he didn't end up landing the gig. Worse, the guy who did win a spot on the tour wasn't a superior musician. He was, however, a die-hard fan of the legend in question and could recount said legend's entire song catalog from memory. Lewis, on the other hand, was a casual fan but didn't know nearly as much about the legend's career or, for that matter, about rock music in general. When I asked Lewis if he would change anything were he to be granted a "do-over" and allowed to audition again, his answer was that he would have read more articles about the legend's career and updated his iPod before he got on the plane.

Talent alone won't land you gigs. You also need to be "in the know." Your chances of scoring a great job will increase exponentially if you are able to showcase wide-ranging industry appreciation and knowledge during your interview. Read up on all the publications and magazines that are relevant not just to the company, but to the industry at large. Before you walk into an interview, you should be able to answer all of the following questions:

- *What are the top five organizations in your industry?*
- *Which organizations are struggling and why?*
- *Who are the top executives/personalities?*
- *What are the three candidates to become the "next big thing"?*
- *What were the biggest newsmakers of the past six months?*

Also, in order to prove that you are not a Tool who lacks knowledge about the world outside of work, you should at the very least be up to speed on the following:

- *The biggest world news stories of the week*
- *The major financial stories of the week*
- *The biggest sports stories of the week* *

Conversational versatility is key to ensuring that you nail every interview you attend. But remember, this isn't "show-and-tell" time. Your interview is not a forum for fact-dropping. Make sure you do your homework, but don't pull a Hermione Granger and get all smug and pretentious if you think you know the right answer.

---

*Sports may be irrelevant in your chosen field, but our country is obsessed with games and you should be prepared to interview with a sports nut. At the very least, you should know who won the last World Series and the Super Bowl. Moreover, it never hurts to have a favorite team. As a default, just pick your college team, or a school or pro team from the town you grew up in. Learn the name of their coach and their star player. Trust me, it will come in handy.

Bond Like Bond . . . James Bond

YOU MIGHT PERFORM WELL IN A SUIT, BUT HOW WELL DO YOU WEAR A DINNER JACKET?

A T SOME POINT during every interview your potential employer(s) will take a long look across the table and silently wonder: "Forget credentials and résumés, who IS this person? How will she/he act when times get tough? How well will she/he represent the company at functions outside the office? Will we enjoy having her/him around?" Unfortunately, you will not have a chance to address this thread of theoretical questioning directly in your interview, yet whether or not you get a job offer may hinge on the perceived answers to such questions. Therefore it is essential that you connect with your interviewer on a personal level during the course of your conversation. You want her/him to leave the interview feeling as if she or he has found the ideal agent for the outfit—someone who is efficient yet engaging, professional yet passionate, versatile and cool under fire. Basically, you want your potential employer to feel like he or she has found their James (or Jane) Bond.

The following are some Bond characteristics that can and should be on display during the interview process:

DINNER PARTY ROYALE

Bond is as comfortable in a dinner jacket as he is in body armor. He is the consummate conversationalist—witty, insightful, and poised. I've spoken with several CEOs who say that one of the key things they look for in new associates is "introduceability," that is, how comfortable would they feel introducing potential candidates at a dinner party? Moreover, how confident would they feel sending a potential candidate to a dinner function as their personal representative? Interviews present you with the opportunity to show potential employers that you can engage as well as execute.

LICENSE AND DESIRE TO KILL

Show your potential employers that you are enthusiastic about your work and are excited about the type of projects they might throw your way. After all, having a license to kill doesn't mean a damn thing if you hate pulling the trigger.

THE WORK IS NOT ENOUGH.

One of Bond's most endearing qualities is his incredible array of leisure interests. Scuba certifications and chess mastery are not (usually) prerequisites for landing a job, but you do want to let your employer know that you are a well-rounded person with interests outside of the office.

In addition, you should try to create opportunities for your interviewers to bring up their personal passions *(example: "I noticed your autographed Tiger Woods glove on the way in. Do you ever get a chance to play golf when you visit the satellite office in Florida?")*. Once you get them talking about their own hobbies, you'll have a great shot at making a personal connection.

NEVER SHAKEN OR STIRRED

James Bond oozes confidence. He isn't loud or in-your-face cocky, but there is never any doubt that he feels up to the task, whatever it may be. His steady gaze, vocal tone, and clear answers all project a self-assurance that is never shaken or stirred.

Confidence is like a banana in your smoothie. You can always tell if it's in there. If you have confidence in yourself and your abilities, the person sitting across the table will notice. However, too much confidence (like too many bananas) will leave a nasty aftertaste once you are finished.

Finally, understand this: Many older executives don't trust our generation. They don't think we're prepared to work as hard as they did. Furthermore, the thought of delegating work to us really freaks them out. It's up to you to prove that you are not one of those whiny, lazy, spoiled, and flighty twentysomethings that people keep writing about in magazines. Show them something they can trust. Show them Bond.

CH. 16

Cry Me a River

REJECTIONS HAPPEN. GET OVER IT AND GET
BETTER.

GETTING REJECTED FOR a job is kind of like wetting your pants on the elementary school bus—more often than not, you get the feeling that something bad is brewing ahead of time, yet that doesn't make the experience any less demoralizing when it goes down. At first, you just sit there, stunned, realizing that you didn't make it the whole way. However, the initial shock soon gives way to embarrassment and self-loathing. Is there something wrong with you? What are your parents going to think? Will your friends judge you? The whole experience stinks.

Shake it off, kid.

Start embracing rejections and (more important) learning from them. I'm not suggesting that you shouldn't be disappointed; that's unrealistic. When I first started shopping book proposals around to literary agents, I got shot down more often than aspiring actors on *ElimiDATE*, and it sucked each time. However, once I got over my ego and started searching for productive critiques within the rejection messages and e-mails, I was able to make the improve-

ments that led to a deal, and subsequently the book you are currently reading.

Rejection is a vital part of the interview process, so you'd better
learn to make the most of it. You can start by doing the following:

ACCEPT IT.

You can't learn from professional rejection until you accept that it
happened, yet many people take great pains to avoid doing so. It
has been my experience that there are three primary strategies for
denying rejection.

1. *Distraction.* The easiest and most common method is to
   run and hide. Once you get the "You're not right for us
   at this time" e-mail, you delete it and get as far away
   from the computer as possible. You go bowling, you
   watch movies, you go to a bar, and then you go to three
   more bars. Anything to take your mind off the fact that
   you just got denied. In the back of your mind you hope
   that if you keep busy enough and kill enough time (and
   Cuervo), you'll forget about the rejection entirely. Dumb
   idea because (a) trying to forget about something is a
   surefire way to ensure that you'll obsess about it, and (b)
   you shouldn't want to forget it in the first place.
2. *Pride protection.* Overachievers, I'm callin' you out. The
   pride protection method is when you tell yourself and
   others that you didn't really try that hard anyway, so
   you're not surprised that you got rejected. Bullshit.
   Whether or not you're telling the truth, the approach is
   bullshit. Get over your "too cool for school" self and admit that you tried. If things didn't go your way, own up
   and move on. Nobody is going to take away your

"Gifted" badge simply because you got turned down once, twice, or even twenty times.

3. *Determined denial.* Some people just don't get it. They decide they want something so badly that when they are rejected, it just doesn't sink in. Rather than electing a new path, they just ram their heads against the same wall over and over again. Remember Stacy from *Wayne's World*?

> Stacy: *Happy anniversary, Wayne.*
> Wayne: *Stacy, we broke up two months ago.*
> Stacy: *Well, that doesn't mean we can't still go out, does it?*
> Wayne: *Well, it does actually. That's what breaking up is.*

Of the three strategies, determined denial is by far the saddest to witness. Once again, you can't learn from rejection until you accept it.

DON'T TAKE "NO" WITHOUT ANSWERS.

Always ask why you didn't get the gig. You hear me? Always. You've got nothing to lose and everything to gain by asking post-rejection questions. It's not like the firm is going to send a Nordic hit man after you for asking too many questions, like Bandini, Lambert and Locke did to Gary Busey in *The Firm*. The worst that could happen is nobody calls you back. Big deal.

The best time to get candid feedback about your self-presentation and performance in interviews is right away, while the whole experience is still fresh in people's minds. Additionally, it is important that you ask direct questions rather than simply "Whaaa happened?"

Get to the root of the issues. You need to know which of the following areas to work on:

1. *Credentials.* Did your résumé undermine your candidacy?
2. *Industry knowledge.* Did you "get" the organization in question?
3. *Q&A.* Did your answers suck? If so, how?
4. *Personality.* This is a tough one to address directly, but in an ideal world it would be good to know if you presented yourself as someone who would be easy to work with, or if you came off as an annoying Tool.

In the event that you get an e-mail rejection, look in the body of the message for clues about why you came up short and then probe those areas in a follow-up e-mail.

GET OVER IT.

Don't let rejections slow you down. Just because you've got some areas to work on doesn't mean that you need to get back on the bench. Use the feedback to improve your game. Schedule more interviews, more networking dinners, and more coffee talks. You can't get better if you don't get more experience.

PART FIVE

Talk the Talk

BECOME A RESPONSIBLE PROFESSIONAL BY
CUTTING BACK ON YOUR BS EMISSIONS.

Shut Up and Say Something, *Apprentice*!

KEEP YOUR RAMBLIN' TO A MINIMUM AT THE OFFICE.

DURING EVERY EPISODE of *The Apprentice* (that I watched), Donald Trump stared down underperforming young employees from across the boardroom table and asked pointed questions relating to their failed tasks. Inevitably, at least one wannabe Apprentice felt compelled to launch into a drawn-out monologue justifying his/her poor performance:

> *"Mr. Trump, I don't think we can really feel, like, upset with our performance. Our team all gave 110 percent. The business plan I developed was rock solid and should have been perfect for this challenge. I mean, when we ran over our battle plan last night, I was sure we would sell at least 2,500 baseball cards at the swap meet. Sure, I was a little disappointed when we found out it was going to rain, but I honestly didn't believe weather would, you know, delay the Krump dancers. Furthermore, if Marcus had been able to deliver Derek Jeter like he promised..."*

It made me wonder if the poor schmuck had ever seen the show before. Not once did The Donald ever listen to such a speech and respond by saying, "Thank you for that thorough explanation." Instead he cut the person off mid-sentence and bellowed, "Just answer the question!" followed by, "You're fired," a minute later. Trump didn't have time or patience to waste on rambling novices. Most likely, your boss won't either.

I learned I had a "rambling problem" in humbling fashion a few years back. I had just returned from delivering a very productive client pitch in North Carolina. My boss at the time, Dave, who had just returned from two solid days of grueling meetings in New York, called and asked me to explain how the pitch had gone, so I took a couple minutes to recount the trip. After all, he had used the word "explain." When I finished my very thorough retelling, his response was delayed and emotionless: "Great."

Not the shower of praise I was expecting, but an affirmation at least. He followed with, "Okay, what are our next steps?" I had thought a lot about this as well and went off in detail about several potential courses of action. Occasionally, Dave would throw in an "uh-huh" or "sure" but for the most part he stayed silent. At this point, I should have picked up on the fact that he was waving the universal flag of boredom, but, to be honest, I hadn't quite resolved how I was going integrate all the thoughts I had put on the table.

I didn't realize that I had lost Dave completely until one of my questions was met with dead silence, followed by a gurgling sound and a high-pitched chuckle.

What!!??

It wasn't until I heard Dave laughing in the background that I realized that he had put his two-year-old son, Tad, on the phone while I was in mid-sentence. That's right, I got "toddlered"!

I was stunned, pissed, and confused all at once. Due to this debilitating emotional overload, I couldn't think of anything to say when Dave got back on the phone and told me I should "check back in tomorrow." I immediately ran to the bathroom to grab a Band-Aid for my ego.

The lesson? Enter every professional conversation with a time limit. It doesn't matter if you're in a formal meeting, on the phone, or just popping your head into somebody's office. Respect your colleagues' time by keeping it short and sweet. Nobody wants to listen to you ramble on. The aforementioned toddlering is a case in point. My boss asked me a one-line question and I responded with a five-page answer. I didn't take into account the fact that he had spent the previous two days in heavy meetings and was probably sick of hearing people talk. He just wanted a quick update. Now, does my failure to consider the needs of my audience justify the inexcusably unprofessional act of putting one's toddler son on the phone with a colleague in mid-sentence? Probably not, but that's not the point. I should have just shut up and said something.

Like, Listen to . . . Uh . . . Yourself Talk, Ya Know?

SPEECH "FILLERS" ARE JOB KILLERS.

THE WORD "LIKE" and the phrase "ya know" are called "fillers" because we use them to fill space when we have nothing of substance to say. Instead of pausing for a moment to contemplate what to say next, we unconsciously use fillers to plug the gaps in our sentences. In the process we end up sounding like characters from *The Hills*. Then again, after a few decades of watching MTV it should not come as a surprise that we speak like mall rats from the Valley. Unfortunately, most people don't even recognize that they use and abuse fillers. Our generation has grown so accustomed to mall-speak that we have very little perspective on how obnoxious it is for other/older people to listen to. I don't care how talented, qualified, or personable you are; your chances of landing a cool job and accelerating up the food chain diminish significantly if you talk like Phoebe from *Friends* or the cast of *The O.C.*

I'd like to take a moment to call attention to some specific fillers by profiling their users and abusers.

FILLER #1: "LIKE"

Back in the day, "like" was used to compare and contrast, or to describe affinity for someone or something. That all changed when the Valley Girls invaded. Equipped with surgically enhanced good looks and designer lifestyles, the Valley Girls emerged in droves during the "earn and burn" '80s, inspiring American youth to embrace their inner ditz. All of a sudden "likes" swarmed through the airwaves like locusts. Kids became hooked, yet the government did nothing to combat the culture of abuse. For more than twenty-five years, the plague has continued to spread. Today "like" is commonly tacked on to nearly every part of speech, even itself ("I, like, totally like, like her, dude").

Excessive usage resembles Cher from *Clueless* and makes you sound

   a. *Immature.* As I've explained, "like" is a Gen X/Y addiction. There aren't a lot of people over the age of forty who abuse this filler. Therefore excessive usage of "like" will call attention to your youth and inexperience.

   b. *Inarticulate.* When you abuse "like," others will assume that you lack the vocabulary to properly express yourself. Worse, it's a dead giveaway that you watched "Clarissa Explains It All" and/or "Sabrina the Teenage Witch" when you were younger.

FILLER #2: "UH"

"Uh" does nothing more than kill time while you're thinking of something to say. "Uh" adds absolutely nothing to your sentences; it is as unnecessary as a Hummer in your driveway or a fourth out-fielder in softball. You would be hard-pressed to find an instance in which deployment of an "uh" makes a person sound intelligent.

Excessive usage resembles Lumbergh from *Office Space* and makes you sound
  a. *Unfocused.* "Uh" undermines the strength of any state-ment because it implies that you had to search to find your words. Sadly, "uh" is the most frequently abused filler during meetings and oral presentations. The next time you attend a speech, lecture, etc., try to count the number of times the person at the front of the room says "uh." You'll be amazed.
  b. *Unauthoritative (if that's even a word).* Who inspires more professional confidence, the guy who says, "I left that report on your desk last Tuesday," or the one who says, "I, uh, left that uh, report on your desk, uh, last Tuesday"?

FILLERS #3 AND #4: "SO" AND "YA KNOW"

"So" and "ya know" are the bookend fillers. "So" is often used to announce that one is beginning a sentence (as in: "So, I went to the movies on Saturday"). Why is this necessary? I'm not really sure. One would think that the act of speaking by itself would be enough to indicate that one is about to say something.

"Ya know" on the other hand is most often used at the end or near the end of a sentence or phrase. Sometimes it causes statements to unnecessarily morph into questions and other times it just seeks affirmation.

Excessive usage resembles Marge Gunderson from *Fargo* and makes you sound
  a. *Unsure of yourself.* "Ya know," especially, seems to ask for affirmation whether appropriate or not, as in *"I think our sales projections are totally reasonable, ya know?"*
  b. "So," on the other hand, makes you sound apprehensive about the statement you are about to make, especially when it gets drawn out at the beginning of your sentence, as in *"Sooooo, about those QED reports..."*

FILLER #5: "DUDE"/"MAN"

"Dude"/"Man" abuse starts in much the same way as substance abuse. You start doing it because the "cool people" are doing it. At first you only partake on occasion because there's nothing wrong with a "dude" or "man" amongst friends every now and then. But used in excess, these fillers can inhibit your everyday functionality: *"Man, Karen, those figures really make sense to me now. Nice job, dude."* Left untreated, "Dude"/"Man" abuse can take over your life.

Excessive usage resembles Bill and Ted from *Bill and Ted's Excellent Adventure* and makes you sound
  Dumb (and a little stoned). And if it looks this dumb on paper, then it probably sounds even dumber coming out of your mouth at work.

So, like, uh, listen to yourself talk, ya know, dude? You can't afford to let the substance of what you have to say get overshadowed by mall rat affectations. You need to kick your addiction to verbal fillers . . . and it won't be easy. There aren't any foolproof methods to help you quit—no patches, no support groups, no special chewing gum. In fact, the best advice I can give you is to take a quick breath when you catch yourself using fillers. If you acknowledge (internally) that you slipped, you'll be less likely to do it in the future.

Win Every Staring Contest

CONFUCIUS SAY: "SILENCE IS A TRUE FRIEND THAT
NEVER BETRAYS."

BELIEVE THAT MOST twentysomethings are scared of silence.
Growing up, we were constantly stimulated by noises, whether
from electronic devices or from people, and as a result we are
much more comfortable with sound than we are without it. Television and movies have only served to reinforce the phobia. Think
about it. If you're watching a movie that was made in the '80s or
'90s and there's no sound, for even a second or two, it probably
means that someone is about to take a meat cleaver between the
shoulder blades. Quiet = Death.

Whether or not my overstimulation theory holds water, it is
hard to deny that our generation speaks for the sake of avoiding
silence. Unfortunately, our scatter chatter puts us at a major disad-
vantage in tense professional settings, especially when money is on
the line.

The best negotiators embrace silence and even use it to their
advantage. Not surprisingly, the best professional poker players do
this as well. Consider Annie Duke and Howard Lederer, the leading brother/sister tandem on the professional poker circuit. It

seems as though Annie and Howard are on TV more than the news, an observation that leads me to two conclusions: (1) Poker is on TV way too much; (2) Howard and Annie are damn good poker players. After spending several hours on the couch watching the two of them tear through tournaments, I came to realize the family secret to their success: They win every staring contest.

It's pretty amusing to watch Annie Duke stare down an online poker wizard in dark shades and a trucker hat. She is not mean, just methodical. Before she places a bet, she'll gaze across the table at the poor kid and just tilt her head ever so slightly as if to say: "What are you thinking about, my friend?" She doesn't say a word, just gazes. More often than not, her adversary will make a gesture or muster up a one-liner to break the awkward silence and motivate her to make a move. Maybe he's bluffing or maybe he's got the nuts (best hand) and is worried that she'll fold. Whatever it is, Annie, a former psychology PhD candidate, will likely figure it out. She can read people like *People*, especially when silence makes them mumble.

Howard, on the other hand, is a master of the stone-cold stare down. His nickname is "the Professor" because he aggressively analyzes his opponents during silent staring contests. His gaze is so intense that most players feel compelled to turn away. As with Annie, Howard's opponents usually grow restless and reveal "tells" that betray their positions.

Annie Duke and Howard Lederer have made millions of dollars by winning staring contests, and there's no reason you can't do the same at work. Many of the tactics they employ at poker tables will work at conference tables as well. Become unbeatable in staring contests and you will have a distinct advantage when you go "heads-up" with your boss to negotiate a starting salary or a raise. The more comfortable and confident you are with silence, the stronger you will become in negotiations and tense deliberations.

40-Year-Old Q&A

LESSONS IN BS FROM HOLLYWOOD'S FAVORITE VIRGIN

WE CAN ALL relate to Steve Carell in *The 40-Year-Old Virgin*. Now, before you go getting your undies in a bunch, understand that I'm not challenging the depth or breadth of your mojo. I'm just pointing out that once you take a step back from the sex (or lack thereof), *Virgin* is simply a film about an inexperienced person struggling to get a grip in an experienced world. Andy (Carell) wants to play with the big kids, but he just can't seem to get it together when the pressure is on.

Andy's biggest problem is that he is ashamed of his inexperience. He feels like a lesser person because he's not (for lack of a better phrase) gettin' any. His insecurities become painfully apparent whenever sex or dating comes up in conversation. He becomes visibly nervous and stammers, stutters, and stumbles through his sentences. Andy goes awkwardly out of his way to protect his "secret" and ends up sounding and looking absurd in the process. Luckily, as the movie progresses, Andy realizes that he needs to get over his embarrassment and own up to his inexperience before he can get over the hump (sorry about that one . . .

I couldn't help it) and learn how to interact comfortably with women. Like Andy, many young professionals often talk a big game in order to mask their inexperience-based insecurities. And, like Andy, they end up making things even worse.

In the office, as in the bedroom, there are several reasons that it is productive to own up to one's inexperience before trying to get one's swerve on. For example:

IMPROVISED BS IS TRANSPARENT.

While playing cards with his coworkers in *Virgin*, Andy is asked to share a detailed sexual encounter. Considering that Andy has never had any sexual encounters, he would have been wise to deflect the question or simply decline to answer. Instead he gets nervous and tries to improvise, resulting in the following unconvincing statement: *"You know, when you, like, you grab a woman's breast and it's . . . and you feel it and . . . it feels like a bag of sand when you're touching it?"*

Andy's BS only amplifies his ignorance in front of the group. His coworkers instantly know that he's never felt a breast before—c'mon, bag of sand? He would have been much better off had he just kept his mouth shut. Professional conversations are the same. If you don't have the knowledge or experience necessary to answer a question—whether in a job interview, at a board meeting, or even while conversing casually with your boss—resist the urge to make something up. Why would you risk committing your own "bag of sand" debacle? Think of it like the SATs. If you don't have a clue what the answer is, leave it blank. If you guess wrong, you'll lose points; but you neither gain nor lose points for omitting an answer.

BETTER TO TAKE YOUR MEDICINE NOW . . .

When you start spitting BS, sooner or later you're gonna get screwed (not like that, you perv). Actually, the best-case scenario is that you'll get called out early, like Andy with the "bag of sand" comment. The worst thing that can happen is that people will accept your BS answer and then follow up with additional questions. Naturally, you'll feel compelled to spout more BS in order to cover up your initial BS. Next thing you know, you'll be overstressed, overwhelmed, and scrambling for your life like Leonardo Di-Caprio in *The Aviator* or Christina Applegate in *Don't Tell Mom the Babysitter's Dead*.

Actually, I think the 2003 movie *Shattered Glass* provides the best Hollywood example for this section. Based on a true story, the movie follows a twentysomething journalist, Stephen Glass, who is so desperate to make a name for himself as a journalist that he conjures up fake news stories. At first the BS pays off and several of Stephen's stories get published in *The New Republic*. However, as the movie progresses, his lies pile up like pizza boxes in a frat house until it becomes blatantly obvious to everyone around that something stinks. In the end Stephen loses his credibility, his job, his friends, and so forth.

Don't let your insecurity shatter your professional credibility. Tell the truth and keep it real.

PEOPLE LIKE TO TEACH.

When Andy finally confesses his virginity to his girlfriend, Trish, he is surprised to learn that she is totally cool with his inexperience. Turns out, Trish is happy to take on the roll of experienced instructor and embraces the opportunity to teach Andy some tricks of the trade. It's fun for her. Him, too (duh).

The sooner you embrace your inexperience, the sooner you will find a willing instructor or two to show you the ropes. In fact, I'd wager that most of your coworkers will jump at the chance to play professor. It will make them feel wanted and valuable. And, like Andy, it will give you the best opportunity to sharpen your skills.

PART SIX

The Road to Stardom

PAY YOUR DUES, FOLLOW THROUGH, STAND
OUT, AND MOVE UP.

Make It Work, Designers!

SPEND LESS TIME QUESTIONING THE CHALLENGE AND MORE TIME BATTLING THROUGH IT.

TIM GUNN, THE impeccably dressed mentor on Bravo's fashion-favorite hit *Project Runway*, is not unlike several bosses I've worked for in the past. He is an opinionated middle-aged guy with a propensity for nonchalantly issuing absurd orders that send the entire office into a state of complete chaos. For example, Gunn might kick off an episode of *Runway* with the following:

> *"Good morning, Designers! I'm sure that most of you are probably wondering why we dragged you out of bed at 4 a.m. and brought you to McDonald's. Here's the deal: Your next challenge is to design and construct a tasteful and professional, yet fashion-forward pantsuit for the modern woman using only McMuffin wrappers, hairnets, and Happy Meal prizes. Workstations have been set up for you outside in the Playland. You have eight hours to complete this challenge. Make it work, designers!"*

"Make it work." That's the only advice Tim offers the designers before retreating off the set. After all, there isn't really much more he can do. Is he aware that the fashion designers would like more time to complete their tasks? Sure he is. Does he recognize how absurd most of the challenges are? You bet. Unfortunately, he doesn't have the authority to change any of the parameters. He may be an expert and (some would argue) an icon in the fashion world, but Tim doesn't call the shots on *Runway*, the producers do. All Tim can do is check in from time to time, offer productive critiques and words of encouragement, and make sure that the designers are on track to submit something at the end of the day. When you think about it, Tim Gunn is the show's middle manager.

As for the designers, they whine and complain but not for too long—they don't have time to waste bitching while they're stitching. They know that each challenge has winners who get promoted and losers who get cut. No matter how successful they've been in the past, they can't afford to slack off. Even if they can't produce their best work they still have to produce something, lest they find their heads on the chopping block.

Take away the Happy Meal toys and hairnets and *Project Runway* challenges aren't much different from everyday office fire drills. When faced with absurd tasks and impossible deadlines, some kick it into high gear and face the challenge head-on, while others say "screw it" and pack it in. If you want to be the last one standing, you've got to make it work. You can't afford to send crap down the runway.

Jessica Simpson and Becoming *Employee of the Month*

SUCCESS IN MULTITASKING IS BASED ON QUALITY, NOT QUANTITY.

JESSICA SIMPSON WAS on fire in 2004. With a chart-topping album as well as a hit reality show, *Newlyweds*, on MTV with her boy band husband (now ex-husband), Nick Lachey, Jessica finally emerged from behind the shadow of Britney and Christina as Hollywood's "it" ditz. America couldn't get enough of Jessica's talent, beauty, or daily struggles with simple household appliances. Naturally, like countless celebs before her, Jessica sought to capitalize on her star power and load up on as many new projects as she could pronounce.

By 2005 it was tough to turn on the television without seeing the results of Jessica Simpson's blonde ambition. She sang the national anthem at major sporting events, pitched name-brand jeans, starred in an awful remake of *The Dukes of Hazzard*, yet still found time to hype her kid sister, Ashlee, and hawk acne medication on late-night infomercials. She and Nick even had their own '70s-style network variety show. Yes, Jessica seemed to be an unstoppable multimedia force.

Unfortunately, Jessica soon discovered what happens when you overload your plate. She became overextended, overexposed, and generally overwhelmed. By early 2006 Jessica's record sales had slowed, her acting had been panned by critics, her marriage had crumbled, and she had been hit with a $100 million lawsuit from Tarrant Apparel Group (TAG), the company that manufactured her name-brand jeans, "Princy." Apparently, she failed to actively promote TAG brands and even snubbed Princy jeans in the media by identifying another brand as her favorite. Not a smart move.

Jessica may have aspired to become the *Employee of the Month* in the aptly named 2006 movie, but if you follow her professional example you will never earn that title yourself. As the number of projects on your desk increases, so does the probability that you won't complete any of them to any degree of satisfaction. Anyone can take on six projects, but finishing one task—and finishing it well—takes significantly more determination, focus, and skill.

When you start a new job, you will no doubt enter the office every day bursting with energy and ready to please, like a puppy that's been let out of his crate after a long night, or like Reese Witherspoon in *Election*. Dead set on proving your worth, you will be inclined to say "yes" to every request that comes your way. What better way to learn about a business than to get involved in a little bit of everything, right? Perhaps, but don't take on more than you can handle. Only offer to help with extra projects or assignments if your own responsibilities have already been taken care of.

I know this may sound strange, but I believe we can all learn a lot from Jessica Simpson. Multitasking is a necessary skill for every budding business mogul, but the ability to follow projects through to their conclusion is more valuable. Remember, you only get credit for jobs that get finished, not the ones you attack half-assed or leave untouched on your plate. Know when to say no. Admitting that your plate is full does not make you a slacker. Taking on tasks and not completing them does.

L-L-L-Let's Get Ready to Specialize!

CARVE OUT A NICHE OR SPECIALTY AT WORK THAT MAKES YOU INDISPENSABLE.

MICHAEL BUFFER IS the ultimate specialist. I can't think of anyone else on the planet who has been more successful at developing a specific skill and carving out a niche for himself than the ring announcer from Philadelphia. For more than twenty years Buffer has traveled the globe and kickstarted championship fights with his trademark "L-L-L-L-LET'S GET READY TO RUMB-L-L-L-L-L-E!" In fact, no fight can truly be considered a "Main Event" unless Michael Buffer is there to open the show. He is arguably the most identifiable figure in combat sports, yet he is not a fighter, trainer, referee, or even promoter. Think about that for a second. Can you think of anyone else in the world who serves as the voice of an industry yet participates in only 1/1000th of the activity? Buffer gets paid ridiculous sums of money to perform a ridiculously simple task. What a brilliant businessman!

Michael Buffer didn't set out to take over the world twenty-five years ago, but he did set out to specialize. And, as *Napoleon Dyna-*

mite taught us in 2004, developing sweet skills is key to becoming desirable. Consider the following:

SPECIALIZING ENHANCES YOUR IMAGE.

Specializing will allow you to add a new dimension to your image at work. Remember the *Teenage Mutant Ninja Turtles* (the original cartoon from the '80s, not the computer-generated crap remake that plagued movie screens in 2007)? If the Turtles hadn't specialized, their individual identities would have been tied exclusively to the colors of their respective headbands. Luckily they all had niches. Leonardo led, Donatello did machines. Raphael was "cool but rude" (and he wonders why he was the least memorable turtle. What kind of specialty is "cool but rude"?), and Michelangelo was a party dude. Additionally, each turtle mastered a different weapon that was beneficial not only to him individually but also to the group. For example, if enemies attacked in close quarters, Raphael could stick them with his Sai,* while Donatello could keep dangerous foes at bay (or pole-vault) with his Bo Staff.

Here's a real-world example: When I worked in merger and acquisition integration after college, my boss asked me to research firms that specialized in analyzing organizational culture. Instead of just going on the Internet and checking out a couple of Web sites, I bought books on organizational culture, called companies that had utilized cultural assessment tools and surveys in the past, and dug up dirt on all of the leading niche consultancies. Shortly after presenting my findings, I was asked to set up the cultural assessment phase of a multimillion-dollar acquisition integration.

From then on I became known around the office as "the culture

---

*Sai are old Chinese weapons that resemble large daggers.

guy" and was asked to give presentations to other departments in the company. What's more, because I was dedicating so much time to the culture project, I was allowed to drop a few less desirable tasks (database management among them), which proved to be invaluable for my job satisfaction and daily demeanor.

WATCH OUT FOR ORGANIZATION-SPECIFIC SKILLS.

When selecting a skill or specialization to develop, make sure that it is applicable to an entire industry and not just to your current organization. As "Red" from *The Shawshank Redemption* found out, putting too much stock in organization-specific skills can be crippling when you get back out on the open market. At Shawshank prison, Red (Morgan Freeman) was the big man on campus because he "knew how to get things." If you were doing twenty to life and you wanted a poster or some chewing gum to lighten your mood, Red was the man to call. Unfortunately, all of Red's skills were useless on the outside. In the free world, most people don't need help acquiring porn or cigarettes–they just go to their local convenience store. So, when Red was paroled after forty years in the joint, his specialty was useless. Don't go out like Red. Insulate yourself from the dangers of change by developing specialties with mass appeal.

YM I Out of the Spotlight?

KEEP EARLY SUCCESS IN PERSPECTIVE TO AVOID THE "TOO HOT TOO SOON" HEARTTHROB SYNDROME.

TODAY'S HEARTTHROB IS tomorrow's bitter has-been. Happens all the time. One minute the young guy with the killer curls and deep dimples is featured in pullout posters in every teenybopper magazine (see: *Seventeen*, *YM*, and *BOP* back in the day*). Then before you know it, he's proselytizing on late-night cable (see: Kirk Cameron). Same thing happens in business. One minute one of your peers will be anointed the hotshot of the month by senior management. Then, in the blink of an eye, he'll be serving up chai lattes at Starbucks and serving up antiestablishment blog entries from his apartment.

You need to keep premature success in perspective. Make sure your head doesn't grow too big so you can avoid the following pitfalls:

---

*Gotta take a second and give a shout-out to my wife, Sarah, whose knowledge of '80s/'90s teenybopper magazines vastly exceeds my own. Would you believe that I didn't even know what *BOP* was until she told me about it? Oh ma God!

TAKING YOURSELF TOO SERIOUSLY

Isaac, Taylor, and Zac Hanson were the undisputed teen princes of 1997. Riding the strength of their bubblegum single "MMM-Bop," Hanson rocketed to the top of the pop charts...and promptly sketched out the entire country. To be fair, the boys from Oklahoma weren't sketchy in a "criminally insane cousin-daters" kind of way. Quite the contrary, in fact. The Hansons were well-behaved and well-spoken. Unfortunately they took themselves way too seriously and were way too eager to be older. I'm not just talking about the fact that they got married in their teens, either. The Jenga moment for me was when Hanson released an "early years" album in 1998. How pretentious is that? No band should be allowed to release an early years album if

a. they only have one hit album to date.
b. they are still too young to drink. When *Three Car Garage: Indie Recordings 1995–1996* was released in 1998, the Hanson brothers were seventeen, fifteen, and twelve years old, respectively.

Just because you achieve senior-level success and make senior-level bank doesn't mean that you should start acting like a senior citizen. Young professionals who take themselves too seriously and refuse to act their age are incredibly annoying, not to mention Toolish. Don't let a little success turn you into a holier-than-thou douchebagalow.

FOCUSING ON THE ATTENTION AS OPPOSED TO THE WORK

Attention is addictive, even for seemingly stable stars. In 1994 Jared Leto was the hottest young heartthrob on the block. As Jordan Catalano on *My So-Called Life*, Jared was on the minds and bedroom walls of every teenage girl from Long Beach to Long Island. With dreamy eyes and a signature "serious face" that would make even Luke Perry jealous, Jared seemed destined for superstardom. Unfortunately, when *So-Called* was so canceled, his popularity waned. That is not to say that Jared fell off the map, because he has had an unquestionably successful career. Over the past ten years, he has worked consistently and landed roles in quality films like *Fight Club*, *Requiem for a Dream*, and *American Psycho*. Unfortunately for Jared, none of the roles awarded him Jordan Catalano–level attention.

To be fair, Jared did not have a high-profile meltdown. No public coke binges, no hookers, no arrests of note, and no twenty-four-hour marriages. For a while I assumed that the next time we would hear from Jared Leto (the leading man) it would be in a Patrick Dempsey–style comeback role. Then I got wind of Thirty Seconds to Mars.

In 2006 Jared began turning up on the scene once again, this time as the lead singer of an up-and-coming rock band dubbed Thirty Seconds to Mars. Curious, I hit the Internet to check out some interviews. Jared's quotes indicated he was hungry to evolve as a musician, but his fingerless gloves and excess mascara suggested he was starving for attention.

It seemed as if Jared spent more time trying to get into *US Weekly* than he did refining his lyrics. His spat with Elijah Wood at a party in October 2006 provided final confirmation that he was longing for the limelight. Nothing says "please notice me" like starting some shit with Frodo Baggins when you're thirty-five years old.

Don't go chasing the paparazzi. Focus on the work, not the spotlight.

WONDERING WHERE ALL THE LOVE HAS GONE

In *The Devil Wears Prada*, Andy (Anne Hathaway) lands a job out of college that a million other girls would kill to have. As second assistant to the editor-in-chief of *Runway Magazine* (a fictional *Vogue*), Andy gains elite access to the biggest names, swankiest events, and hottest clothes in the industry. A couple months into the job, however, Andy nearly quits because she feels overworked and underappreciated by her tyrannical boss, Miranda Priestly. Despite the fact that Andy works productively and efficiently for more than eighty hours every week and manages to pull off the near impossible tasks thrown her way, Miranda hardly seems to notice and certainly never offers a word of praise.

Luckily for Andy, a colleague, Nigel (Stanley Tucci), talks some sense into her before she bolts. In the big leagues, he explains, gold stars and hugs aren't awarded when homework is handed in. Nigel tells Andy that she needs to adjust her expectations and recognize that the growth and advancement opportunities afforded to her on a daily basis are worth much more than pats on the back.

You need to develop a professional attitude for the professional world, and part of that development involves learning to subsist on the self-satisfaction of doing your job well. If you feel you can't survive without standing ovations, by all means quit your job, head back to your parents' basement, and let your mom bring you Teddy Grahams while you surf monster.com.

Second Opinions and the Soul Patrol

MAKE SURE MORE THAN ONE JUDGE EVALUATES YOUR PERFORMANCE AT WORK.

DURING SEASON FIVE of *American Idol*, Taylor Hicks taught more than thirty million people about the value of second opinions. For the first two months of the season, Taylor was the recipient of extremely fierce criticism from America's favorite British import, Simon Cowell. From the get-go, Simon didn't believe that this gray-haired, awkward-dancing, soul-singing white dude had a prayer of succeeding on America's most popular talent show. Week in and week out he ripped into Taylor, likening his performances to bad karaoke and comparing his dance moves to those of somebody's drunk uncle at a wedding. By week five, Taylor was almost universally viewed as a million-to-one long shot.

But Taylor took the words of Lloyd Christmas from *Dumb & Dumber* to heart: "So you're sayin' there's a chance."

Instead of wilting under Simon's intense scrutiny, Taylor sought second opinions. He focused on the constructive criticism from *Idol*'s lieutenant judges, Randy Jackson and Paula Abdul, and used it to improve his performances every week. Taylor stayed upbeat and began carving out a spot in the collective hearts of *Idol* viewers and voters. In the season finale, Taylor "soul-patrolled" his way to the Idol crown and even won over Sinister Simon.

Young professionals often put too much stock in the opinion of one colleague, boss, or mentor, thus deriving their entire sense of self-worth and accomplishment from a single source. Corporate Tools, especially, worship their leaders like drag queens worship Cher. Not healthy. I don't care how credible, smart, talented, or famous said supervisor is; she/he has biases and bad days, both of which can affect her/his assessment of your performance. You can't afford to let one negative review chip away at your self-esteem or slow down your career.

Here's another example from the entertainment world. In 1993, Sean Combs (aka Puff Daddy aka P.Diddy aka Diddy) was fired from his job at Uptown Records. The man who fired him, Andre Harrell, was one of the hottest execs in the recording business. Harrell's instincts and decision-making skills were revered throughout the industry (he was later appointed president of Motown Records at the age of thirty-five). Had Puffy accepted the "expert" opinion that he was too cocky and immature to succeed, and tucked his tail between his legs, he never would have evolved into the multiplatinum bad boy mogul he is today. Think about it— no B.I.G., no Sean John, no *Making the Band*, and no "white parties" in the Hamptons. Luckily, Puffy sought a second opinion.

Color Me Bored

STAY BUSY ENOUGH TO AVOID "BUSYWORK."

THE FIRST TIME my boss asked me if I wanted to do some coloring, I was twenty-three years old. It was a Thursday morning and I had finished all of my assignments for the week, so I walked into his office and asked what else I could do.

"Give me a second," he said, not bothering to look up as he put the finishing touches on an e-mail.

"No problem," I said as I accidentally knocked a signed golf ball off of his end table. My boss looked up from his computer, obviously annoyed but trying not to show it.

"So you finished that report yet?" he asked.

"Check your in-box," I answered.

"Great." For a moment he just stared at me, annoyed and confused, until finally a light went on in his head. "Hey, I got it. Why don't you go back to your cubicle and do some coloring? I could use a new picture for my wall. How's that sound, buddy?"

Confused, I watched him reach into his desk and pull out a shiny new box of 64 Crayolas along with a couple sheets of light blue construction paper. I said nothing. He walked out from behind his desk to hand me the materials and usher me out of his office.

"I'll come get you when it's time for mac and cheese."

Okay, so I made the last part up. My boss didn't really hand me crayons and construction paper, but he might as well have. To be honest, I don't remember exactly what he asked me to do. Most likely he sent me off to spice up an organizational flow chart on PowerPoint or do some "competitive research" on the Internet. The specifics are irrelevant, anyhow. My boss just wanted me to get out of his office and do something–anything–productive with my time. That way he could feel like he was actively managing my activities and I would be occupied and leave him alone. Whatever. I ended up wasting the next day and a half on "busywork," the grown-up equivalent of coloring books.

My definition of busywork is as follows: *Any task or set of tasks that do not and will never add significant value to a given organization nor contribute to the professional development of the employee to whom said tasks were assigned.* Busywork eats up time as opposed to objectives. Countless young professionals have lost entire weeks to unimportant spreadsheets, senseless "research projects," and random errands that were dreamed up by their superiors on a whim.

As an ambitious and productive person, you have every right to resent meaningless assignments that find their way to your desk. Recognize, however, that you can't blame anyone but yourself. Busywork is extremely preventable. Here are some suggestions:

STOCKPILE "RAINY DAY" PROJECTS.

You should view lulls in the action as opportunities to develop your own pet projects. There is a point early in the movie *Ray* when Ray Charles's career nearly grinds to a halt. Just as Ray is getting ready to set out on the road in 1954, the headliner gets pregnant and the tour gets called off. The executives at Ray's label don't know what they are going to do with him. Luckily, Ray doesn't wait to find out. Instead of killing time until the execs can find something for him to do, Ray puts together some new material with a full band and convinces the label to let him become the tour's headliner himself.

Make the most of slow periods at work by using the time to research some new ideas, initiate some new projects, or throw together some new material of your own.

RECOGNIZE AND APPRECIATE THE DIFFERENCES BETWEEN "BUSYWORK" AND "NECESSARY TASKS THAT HAPPEN TO SUCK."

There are a slew of administrative tasks (data entry, expense reporting, etc.) that may feel like busywork, but in reality are necessary tasks that happen to suck. Necessary tasks that happen to suck are not intellectually challenging or interesting but they are important. Consider such tasks your chores. Accept them graciously and complete them thoroughly. No one is entitled to interesting work at all times, especially young guns. Young employees who act as though they are doing the boss a favor when in fact they are just doing their chores are appropriately viewed as "spoiled overachievers."

PART SEVEN

Succeeding in Meetings

Produce Your Shows Like the Pros

PREP FOR YOUR MEETINGS LIKE A HOLLYWOOD PRODUCER AND YOU'LL PACK THE HOUSE.

F YOU WANT your meetings and presentations to be successful, you have to entice and captivate your audience. Start thinking like a producer. If you prepare for your meetings and presentations as though they were Hollywood or Broadway premieres, you will put butts in the seats and keep them glued down. Here are a few ideas to get you started:

RECRUIT A SENIOR COPRODUCER.

As a relative unknown in the business, you should target an executive partner to coproduce your meetings and presentations—someone who can serve as an advisor and lend his or her name and credibility to the event. Once you are able to claim that your meeting is being put on "in association with" a senior exec or two, the meeting will become a can't-miss event. Did you ever see *Hustle & Flow*, the 2005 film that made Terrence Howard a star and earned Three 6 Mafia an Oscar? It took years to get that movie produced. Nobody wanted to invest in Craig Brewer, the unknown writer and director of the film. However, once Brewer convinced John Singleton (the accomplished producer behind *Boyz n the Hood*) to join the project, *Hustle* started flowin'. The rest is history.

When you start soliciting senior execs to coproduce your meetings, make it clear to them that you will take care of all the heavy lifting (i.e., do all the work). Also prepare an outline ahead of time so that your potential partners get a clear idea of what they are signing on to.

CAST WELL.

Don't tell me that you're planning on being the only act in your show. You know what I call a one-man show? A lecture, that's what. And you know what I call a lecture? Boring. You need a cast of characters to perform in your meeting/presentation to add color and variety. More important, however, you should dish out a few speaking parts to ensure that more people have a stake in the game. Remember elementary school musicals? For every kid who got a part, there was one more mom willing to sew costumes, and another dad to work on the set (or vice versa . . . settle down). And at least six more tickets would be purchased (God forbid that stepparents, siblings, or in-state second cousins miss out on little Charlotte's rendition of "Somewhere Over the Rainbow"). That said, not every kid in the play needs a solo.

There are several ways to involve colleagues without giving them central speaking roles. For example, you can put someone in charge of designing the presentation template or producing agendas and outlines. You could also ask a colleague to take charge of all the technology (computers, video screens, etc.) that might be used. Just make sure you don't overcast the show or your meeting could end up chaotic and disorganized. There's no reason for your presentation to come off like a low-budget rap concert, with tertiary players wandering aimlessly around the stage with mics, yelling "Awww yeah!" every so often.

DISTRIBUTE THE PLAYBILL.

If people don't have an agenda to follow, their focus will disappear faster than singles at a bachelor party. Send out your agenda in advance to erase any skepticism about the relevance of your meeting.

MAKE TIME FOR A TECH CHECK.

You're going to look pretty dumb if your LCD projector crashes right before your presentation starts. Dry-erase markers and the backup, old-school overhead projector just won't have the same effect. Here are a couple things you should always do to guard against tech failure: (1) Book your venue for an hour before your meeting starts. That should give you enough time to make sure all the equipment you need is set up, and that it all works. (2) If anyone else is going to be submitting materials, slides, or anything else to your presentation, make them submit them to you the night before. You don't need someone else's sloppiness or laziness bringing down your show.

MANAGE THE STAGE.

Don't let your agenda get railroaded by unimportant side conversations or long-winded participants. Four years ago, while working for a real estate investment company in the Bay Area, I wrote and produced an investor presentation designed to raise money for a few of our projects. I knew that all three speakers were likely to run over their allotted time limits like monster trucks, so I actually wrote out "5:00," "1:00," and ":30" time cards so they'd know when to shut it off. A little extreme, you say? Maybe, but the presentation was a success and raised millions of dollars from investors.

FORGET INTERMISSION.

Unlike a Broadway show, you should go out of your way to prevent having a significant intermission, unless your meeting runs longer than three hours. Business audiences are never the same during act 2. In the event that a lunch or bathroom break is inevitable, keep it short to avoid losing attendees to cell phone calls and e-mail diversions.

Conference Table Commandments

TEN LESSONS FOR PROVING YOU BELONG AT THE GROWN-UPS' TABLE

WHEN I WAS a kid, everyone in my family—grandparents, aunts, uncles, and cousins—would converge on our house every Thanksgiving to demolish a turkey. Since my parents never owned a table large enough to seat twenty people, they, like many American families, set up a separate table for all the kids. When I was little, the kids' table was the place to be—no boring conversations, no fancy tablecloths to worry about, a favorable ratio of mashed potatoes to vegetables, and so forth. With every passing year, however, the kids' table became less and less appealing. Before long I was ready to start talking sports and sneaking occasional sips of wine at the grown-ups' table. Before I graduated from the kids' table, however, my mom sat me down and explained the responsibilities that would accompany my new seat. Basic stuff, really—no armpit farts, say "please" and "thank you," stick around until everyone is done eating, blah blah blah. Basically, I needed to prove that I belonged.

Conference tables aren't so different from Thanksgiving tables. If you want to be viewed as a competent executive (as opposed to a "junior nobody") in meetings, you need to play the part and mind your manners. Here are a few tips that will help you prove you belong at the grown-ups' table.

1. **Be on time.** Unless you get abducted by aliens like Homer Simpson in a Halloween special, there is simply no reason to be late. Show up on time (if not early), grab a choice seat, and take a "Moment of Zen" like they do on *The Daily Show*.

2. **Leave your baggage at the door.** Forget about your problems outside of the conference room and focus. If you've got massive distractions in your life that will prevent you from staying attentive during the meeting (see: Luke Wilson in *My Super Ex-Girlfriend*), try to reschedule or get someone else to cover for you.

3. **Understand the totem pole.** Approach the meeting like a backroom dinner on *The Sopranos*. Look around the table and make sure you know who everybody is and where they stand in the family. Furthermore, know your place as well. You don't want to get whacked for speaking out of turn or offending a "made" guy.

4. **Don't apologize for putting your elbows on the table.** Too many young professionals say "I'm sorry" instinctively like Tai in *Clueless* (before her makeover). If you make a comment that isn't perfectly timed, just let it go. Don't draw more attention to yourself with a weak apology.

5. **"How soon will I have all my credit cards paid off? I'll have to get back to you on that, Dad."** If you don't know the answer to a question, use delay tactics rather than making something up.

6. **"It's kind of like what Uncle Steve was saying about spearfishing after dark . . ."** Try to make state-

ments that refer back to what others have said or done. People perk up when they hear their names and will likely stay engaged throughout the conversation. Plus it shows you've been paying attention.

7. **"So, Grandpa, aren't you a little bit worried about the health risks associated with becoming a cage fighter?"** If you hear an idea or plan that sounds crazy to you, make sure to ask clarifying questions before going negative.

8. **Don't call out your cousins.** No need to create an enemy by making someone look bad in public. Seriously, go check out *American Psycho*. I bet Patrick Bateman's colleagues would have been less inclined to make fun of his business cards had they seen him drag Paul Allen's beat-up body through the lobby of his apartment building.

9. **"I guess producing grandkids could be an interesting project for me. . . . Let's table the issue until I get a chance to confer with my office mate."** Try not to commit to new responsibilities while you are caught up in the emotion and peer pressure of a meeting. Remember the Jessica Simpson chapter?

10. **Don't blow your sister's punch line.** Other people's stories will often trigger bright ideas or salient points you've been meaning to bring up, but that doesn't mean you have the right to cut them off mid-sentence. Hold on to your pearls (of wisdom) until after your colleague's story is finished. Also leave some time for a reaction. Nothing says "I don't care what you're saying" like hijacking someone's laugh track time by starting your own story.

Understanding the *Big* Picture

SOMETIMES IT'S BEST TO DISCARD ASSUMPTIONS AND JUST THINK *BIG*.

N *BIG*, THE 1988 comedy that launched Tom Hanks into superstardom, Josh Baskin skips high school and college and lands in the working world after a magic carnival machine (Zoltar) ages him twenty years overnight. In New York Josh manages to score an enviable job as a product tester at a toy company. Later he earns serious accolades after making an extraordinary impression in an ordinary meeting. His success is directly linked to his ability to look past the details and focus on the big picture. This is how it goes down:

> While sitting in a meeting with a few top execs from the toy company, Josh listens to a presentation about a new toy the company is considering. Paul, the exec who is delivering the presentation, cites stats, figures, and historical data that show a market for the toy in question, a building that transforms into a robot. When Paul finishes his presentation, Josh raises his hand.
> "I don't get it," he says.
> Despite all the facts and figures, Paul never explains why the

toy would be fun for children to play with. Still actually a kid himself, Josh knows that the only thing that's really important when it comes to toys is fun. All the marketing wizardry and distribution efficiency in the world won't make a lick of difference if the toy sucks to play with.

In meetings and presentations, numbers are often used to deflect tough questions in much the same way that submarines deploy decoys to distract torpedoes. Such is the case in this scene from *Big*. Paul's fascination with market reports is distracting the group from the important question: Is the toy fun to play with? Josh wasn't challenging Paul for the purpose of being a jerk; he just wanted an answer to his big-picture question before diving into the details.

(Note: It is not a good idea to patronize new coworkers in your first big meeting [see commandment #8 in the previous chapter]. In this case, we'll give Josh a pass because he missed out on two decades of maturation and social interaction. You, on the other hand, should exhibit more tact.)

Your success in meetings and presentations will be directly related to your ability to read audiences and focus on what really matters. While it is important to show that you have a firm grasp on important facts and figures, don't let the details overshadow the big picture.

PART EIGHT

Keep Your Friends Close

RELATIONSHIP ADVICE FOR THE OFFICE

Survivor **Leadership Skills**

LESSONS FROM REALITY TELEVISION CAN KEEP YOU ON THE ISLAND.

YOUNG PROFESSIONALS CAN learn more about leadership by watching *Survivor* than they can by reading most business magazines. I'm serious about this. *Survivor*, the granddaddy of the reality/game show genre, teaches far more junior-level leadership skills than articles written by people who haven't had to scrap and survive since Michael Jackson was popular. Think about it. On *Survivor*, a dozen strangers are thrown together in a foreign environment. Not only are they asked to build successful teams and guide those teams through a series of absurd challenges and obstacles; they must also remain respected and well-liked or else they'll be subject to backstabbing and subsequently kicked off the island.

On the other hand, most leadership articles are written *for* upper management *by* upper management and focus almost exclusively on running companies and ordering underlings around. As an underling yourself, you could care less about techniques for issuing orders from above. Rather, you need to learn how to lead from *within* the pack, build alliances, and earn immunity from the vicious rumor mill.

For those of you who are still skeptical, I offer up the following profiles of typical *Survivor* winners and losers. See if you can spot the similarities between personalities on the island and personalities in the office.

THE LOSERS

The Antisocial Fishermen

On every season of *Survivor* there are at least one or two people who decide to prove their worth by rigging up a pole out of bamboo and palm fronds, then going off by themselves to fish for six hours a day. These fishermen and -women believe their hard work and role as "provider" makes them invaluable to the group. Unfortunately they never last beyond episode five because while they are off alone fishing, everyone else is building relationships and plotting strategy.

I love when the fishermen get voted off *Survivor*, because they never see it coming. After the tribal verdict is read (usually a landslide) the stunned fisherman will invariably make the impassioned "none of you ungrateful #$%@s will survive without me" speech before stalking off in a huff.

Likewise, in a business setting, some people get so caught up in their own tasks that they lose perspective on how they fit into the goals of the team or the organization as a whole.

The Expert

Just because a person possesses the most skills does not necessarily mean that she/he is the most equipped to lead a team. The "Expert" is a perfect example. Every season on *Survivor*, there is at least one former safari guide, Outward Bound instructor, or scout camp leader with decades of outdoor experience and a know-it-all personality. He/she assumes that because he/she is more experienced in starting fires and identifying animal scat than the car salesman, the dentist, or the shockingly good-looking physical trainer, he/she should order the others around and offer unsolicited "expert" advice.

I remember watching a guy spend an entire episode building a crude shelter on the beach. I think he was a CPA or a tax attorney or something. Anyhow, he was pretty stoked to have built something all by himself... that is until the Expert came by and verbally ripped his efforts to shreds by pointing out all the mistakes made during construction. Needless to say, the criticism was not appreciated or well-timed. In fact, the Expert was voted off immediately after the commercial break.

No one likes a know-it-all. Just because you have skills or experience doesn't mean you have carte blanche to drown your colleagues in unsolicited advice. What's that, you say? You can format million-line spreadsheets with your eyes closed? Good for you. Let people in the office know that they can come to you when they get stuck on an Excel assignment, but don't force your expertise on them. If they want to hear the lectures, they'll enroll in your class.

THE WINNERS

Confidants

The most successful leaders on *Survivor*, as well as in business, know that it is more important to listen well than it is to talk a big game. In stressful and competitive environments, someone who takes the time to consult his/her peers is revered above the Tool who can't get enough of the sound of his or her own voice. While most contestants on *Survivor* will go to sleep early on the nights before major "challenges," the Confidant is the one who will stay up talking with a teammate who misses his family or is deathly afraid of snakes and the dark. The Confidants are hardly ever victimized by the rumor mill because they form genuine relationships that transcend the game. On those rare occasions in which the Confidants are voted off the island, the underlying reason is usually that they were perceived as not being genuine.

In stressful, competitive environments like reality television or the office, emotional leaders are more powerful than self-absorbed alpha dogs.

The Dark Horse

I love it when a competitor who is not viewed as the front-runner comes out of nowhere to dominate a challenge for his/her team. Maybe it's the ninety-pound nerd who is able to hang from a coconut tree for twelve hours, or the ex-con who dominates a puzzle challenge. Either way, the Dark Horse competitor spends most of the early stages of the game feeling out the competition and flying below the radar. He/she doesn't try to take the lead all the time, but when the appropriate challenge presents the opportunity to display a talent, the Dark Horse will turn it on like an engine and stun the competition. Afterward, while devouring the precious chocolate chip cookie reward with teammates, she/he will nonchalantly eschew praise, claiming, "It was nothing, really. I was just helping the team."

Lesson: It is often better to under-promise and overperform. If you are able to pleasantly surprise your peers with your skills or talents, the effect will be greater than if you were bragging ahead of time.

———

Look for these personalities the next time that you're watching *Survivor*–or any other reality show for that matter–and then see if you can spot similar attributes around the office. Odds are you will find that people who are in leadership positions more closely resemble the Confidant than they do the Expert.

You Can Be My Wingman Anytime

ENLIST STRONG ALLIES TO COVER YOUR BACKSIDE.

WHEN *TOP GUN* was released in 1986, America fell in love with the Wingman. The term technically refers to a fighter pilot backing up another by flying slightly behind and to the side (near the wing) of his/her jet when entering enemy airspace. But as soon as Maverick, Goose, and the rest of the boys from Miramar finished fighting commies and spiking volleyballs on the silver screen, the Wingman was instantly adapted in countless areas of popular culture. All of a sudden, Wingmen and -women began providing backup in bars, on sports fields, and in office buildings across the country. A few years ago, Coors Light even launched an ad campaign focused on the social Wingman* and (regrettably) the "Wingdog" as well.

Unfortunately the image and integrity of the Wingman has been tarnished in popular culture. No longer must a Wingman possess the courage to engage the enemy, or the skills to maneu-

---

*Remember, he took one for the team (talked up the annoying friend) so his buddy could live the dream (hook up).

ver his/her jet in battle. Instead it seems that all one must do to be anointed a Wingman is show up and tag along for the ride. What an oversight! When you need backup at the office, you can't settle for a tagalong. You need someone with skill and tenacity. Listen up:

A WINGMAN IS A PILOT FIRST.

Here's the deal: Goose (Anthony Edwards), the loyal best friend with the quick wit and a heart of gold, was *not* a true Wingman. No disrespect to the deceased, but Goose was a career copilot. All he did was sit in the back of the plane and congratulate Maverick on his fancy flying. Without Maverick, Goose might as well have been navigating a cargo plane filled with rubber dog excrement out of Hong Kong.

Iceman (Val Kilmer) was the *real* Wingman in the film. Why? Because to be a good Wingman, you've got to be a damn good pilot in your own right. Iceman was the best of the best. The Gooses (Geese?) of the world are good friends, but when push comes to shove, the person assigned to cover your backside better be able to keep up. When you get assigned a last-minute project or client presentation and need to delegate entire portions to a partner, who are you going to pick? The tagalong who sits in the back of the room crackin' one-liners until you instruct him on what to do, or the pro who gets it done before you have to ask? That's right, you want Iceman.

THE WINGMAN ROLE IS RECIPROCAL.

At the end of *Top Gun*, when all the enemy planes have been shot down or run off, Iceman turns to Maverick and says, "You can be my Wingman anytime." Smiling, Maverick responds, "No, you can be mine." The Wingman role is reciprocal. One week, you'll be the one flying out front, and the next you'll be on the wing. Keep that in mind when you are leading a project, and treat your Wingmen with the respect they deserve. Also make sure that you award credit to your Wingmen in front of your boss—they'll be more likely to do the same for you when the roles are reversed.

A QUALIFIED WINGMAN IS AS AMBITIOUS AND COMPETITIVE AS YOU ARE.

Business is a game, and everyone wants to win. That's why you want the best people working with you on your team. That's also why you need to be on your guard. The professional food chain is shaped like a pyramid and everyone is competing for the same top spots. I'm not suggesting that your Wingmen will be out to subvert your activities (at least not early on in the game); I'm just saying that you shouldn't get so caught up in a particular move that you lose sight of the board.

Vicious Cockfights and the Beers That Follow

DON'T MISS OUT ON POST-BATTLE BONDING OPPORTUNITIES.

AFTER A LONG day at the office or on the road, nothing sounds better to me than takeout and a decent bed... unless people on my team are getting together for a drink. Like soldiers coming off the battlefield or athletes in from the playing field, the best time to bond with coworkers is right after you've all been dragged through the ringer. Post-battle bonding affords you the opportunity to strengthen your relationships by rehashing your shared experiences over a beer, a burger, or some breakfast.

The best cinematic example I can think of to highlight my point is from *Anchorman: The Legend of Ron Burgundy*. Midway through the film, Ron and his news team engage in a violent street brawl with several rival news teams. Punches and tridents are thrown, limbs are lost, and one guy gets set on fire. Luckily, Ron's crew emerges unscathed. Anyhow, the next scene finds Ron and Co. back at the station, sharing a beer and recounting the ordeal. Together they come to grips with everything that transpired (Brick killed a guy, for starters), and Ron commends the fellas for keeping their wits about them during the "vicious cockfight."

Watching the scene, you can almost feel the guys growing closer to each other. Personally, I have never bonded with coworkers after a vicious street brawl. Up to this point in my career, my post-battle bonding with colleagues has been more likely to involve a Denny's Grand Slam after a long night at the office . . . but, hey, it's the camaraderie that counts.

Sometimes it takes a half-asleep, brain-fried field trip for colleagues to let their professional guard down and open up on a personal level. About four years ago, a coworker and I got stuck at Kinko's off the strip in Vegas for six hours, copying and printing brochures for an event the next day. His computer crashed, my cell phone ran out of batteries, and the late-night staff at Kinko's wasn't exactly going out of their way to help us out. When we finally finished at 3:15 a.m., we walked across the street to a gas station, bought microwavable chimichangas, and proceeded to eat them while sitting on the curb. The food was awful and the curb got my pants all dirty, but that moment was more memorable to me than anything else that happened in Vegas that weekend. More important, the experience brought us closer together and from then on we went out of our way to help each other out with projects at work.

Try not to miss out on post-battle bonding opportunities. The hour you spend hanging out after a tough day is much more valuable than that extra hour of sleep you might be passing up.

Friends in Low Places

WHEN YOU CATCH YOUR BIG BREAK, DON'T FORGET ABOUT YOUR *ENTOURAGE*.

N HBO's *ENTOURAGE,* Vince Chase is a young actor who moves from Queens to L.A. and becomes a huge movie star. Unlike many of the newly crowned Hollywood "it" kids, however, Vince doesn't "go Hollywood" by ditching all his friends for models, other young celebrities, and groupies. Instead he stays loyal to his boys from New York, giving them a place to crash and using his celebrity status to help them kick-start their respective careers.

Vince is not a social climber and you shouldn't be either. Social climbers may accelerate up the professional ladder by stepping on their peers and coworkers, but they run the risk of serious injury because nobody at the bottom will stick around to hold the ladder steady. Social climbers do not consider the long-term effects of burning through personal relationships. Selling out your friends for a taste of success will leave you isolated. Not to mention that it makes you a dickhead.

———

If you want to develop and maintain a well-rounded understanding of your organization or industry, you need to develop and maintain relationships with people below as well as above you on the food chain. I don't care if they are answering phones, cleaning bathrooms, or interning for the summer, they still play a role in the company and understand the organization in a unique way. Maintaining access to their perspectives will make you a stronger leader as you move on up. Not to mention that they will remain strong allies for you when they catch a break.

Finally, social climbers have a tough time building up good karma. Why risk it? Follow the example of Vince Chase and stay true to your crew.

CH. 34

Jerky with the Jocks, Nuggets with the Nerds

HANGING OUT WITH EVERY CLIQUE WILL KEEP YOU FROM CATCHING "SILO SYNDROME."

WHEN I WORKED at a Fortune 500 company in Chicago, the cafeteria often resembled a high school lunchroom. The athletes grunted loudly at one table while the nerds giggled nervously across the way. The theater kids sat on top of their table (so as not to conform), and the popular girls pretended to eat their Caesar salads. Okay, so maybe I'm confusing it with a scene from *Mean Girls*, but you get what I'm talking about. People didn't venture outside of their departments.

Business literature often refers to this isolationist behavior as "silo syndrome." Personally, I think the farm reference is a little dramatic, so I just call it "company cliques." After all, when departments and business units can't communicate frequently or openly with one another, it's just like they're back in high school. Each department loses sight of its context and relative importance within the greater organizational landscape, like power-tripping yearbook staffers who believe that seniors shouldn't be able to graduate if they fail to fill out their "most likely to" surveys.

Cliques cause a variety of problems and create unhealthy rivalries. Competition for financial resources intensifies, and suspicion concerning the activities, motives, and productivity levels of competing divisions permeates the organization. Instead of focusing on what can be done to become innovative in the marketplace and get a jump on the competition, departments will concentrate on getting a leg up internally, thereby fostering a corporate culture ripe with distrust and ulterior motives.

DANNY OCEAN AND THE "HAVING A GUY" MENTALITY

In order to avoid becoming cliquish yourself, make sure you switch lunch tables once in a while. For your own advancement, you should also try to eat dinner with kids from a different school every now and then as well. The more you venture outside of your immediate clique, the more likely you are to develop your own network of "guys." In this case I'm not talking about getting guys like a high school cheerleader gets guys. Rather, I'm talking about getting guys like Danny Ocean from *Ocean's Eleven* gets guys. When Danny Ocean needs to blow the door off a casino vault, he gets on the phone and calls his "dynamite guy." When he needs someone small and flexible enough to squeeze into a chip cart and get smuggled into the vault, he just dials his "Chinese contortionist guy." Personally, I don't have a "Chinese contortionist guy," but I do have a "Web guy," a "finance guy," and a "bookkeeping gal." Each one of them makes my life easier.

I block out time every week to go meet new people, because I subscribe to the theory that one can never have too many "guys." Danny Ocean obviously agrees with me because he adds a "new guy" in every sequel.

(By the way, I fully expect that my unborn children will buy tickets to see *Ocean's 24* when they are in high school. By that time, the gang will probably be knocking off virtual casinos from their nursing home La-Z-Boys in Palm Springs. Ah, but I digress once again....)

Find a Miyagi Mentor

SEEK OUT ACCOMPLISHED AND PATIENT MENTORS
TO HELP YOU DEVELOP YOUR SKILLS.

DO YOU EVER watch "mentor movies"? You know, films in which a central story line is built around the evolution of a student/teacher relationship. The vast majority of kung fu films (or films starring Al Pacino) fall into this category. Settings change, but the story line is almost always the same. A young girl (or guy) whose life is moving slower than anticipated rolls into town with a big bag of clothes and some untapped potential. She (or he) wanders through various dead-end activities for a few scenes before bumping into a mysterious mentor who "sees something" in her and offers to show her the ropes. Fifteen minutes and several training montages later, the young woman emerges as a ninja, world-class spy, or slick business tycoon.

There are generally two movie mentor types: the "protégé-seeking mentor" and the "self-serving mentor." In this chapter I will identify the differences between the two mentor types, in film and at work, by examining relationships in *The Karate Kid* and the *Kill Bill* movies.

THE PROTÉGÉ SEEKERS

Protégé seekers are accomplished mentors whose careers have already peaked. Having gone through the trials and tribulations of ascension themselves, they are eager to pass on their wisdom to younger generations. Mr. Miyagi from the *Karate Kid* movies is a great example.* Demanding yet patient, tough yet supportive, Mr. Miyagi helps Daniel-san LaRusso unlock his potential and become a world-class martial artist. Though he was a superstar in his own right, Miyagi is quite eager and excited to pass along the tricks of the trade to the next generation.

Once you identify a Miyagi mentor to help you in your career, you need to prove that you are committed to working hard and developing as a student ("wax on, wax off"). Good mentors don't waste their time on pupils with potential but no work ethic. As Miyagi said: "Either you karate do 'yes' or karate do 'no.' You do karate 'guess so' (*makes squish gesture*) just like grape. Understand?"

That's some deep s#@t right there.

SELF-SERVING MENTORS

Self-serving mentors seek to control their students and exploit their talents for personal gain. Personal development is nurtured only as long as the student does the teacher's bidding. (These mentors will teach their birds to sing, but they don't want them leaving the cage.) Such was the case in *Kill Bill* (volumes 1 and 2). In the story, Bill, a master assassin, falls in love with one of his

---

*The first *Karate Kid* movie was made in 1984, making this one of the oldest references in the book. If you weren't born yet, go get the DVD. It's a frickin' classic. Do it, do it.

pupils, Beatrix Kiddo. When Bill learns that Beatrix has left him and moved on with her life, he flips out, crashes her wedding, kills her entire wedding party, and shoots her in the head.

Self-serving mentors view students who advance too quickly as threats and therefore will often take steps to ensure that their students are "held back" from achieving too much autonomy. In the working world, this can be achieved through a number of actions—limiting access to superiors, assigning low-exposure tasks, taking credit for the student's work, or simply over-critiquing work in order to discourage self-confidence.

Beware! Self-serving mentors are even sneakier and harder to detect in real life than in the movies. They will most likely mask their evil intentions and feign friendship with their pupils, opening doors of opportunity only so long as they are able to lead the way through. By the time the student realizes the mentor's true intentions, she/he will have lost valuable time—and confidence—which makes the task of challenging her/his master even more daunting.

When it comes to picking mentors, you need to be smart. Before you hitch your wagon to an experienced teacher, conduct a background check. How has he/she treated previous mentees? Does he/she have a history of developing talent? What are his/her personal career goals and how will that affect your development? Seek out a mentor who will force you to work hard but also respect your right to grow autonomously. As Miyagi says: "Better learn balance. Balance is key. Balance good, karate good. Everything good. Balance bad, better pack up, go home. Understand?"

White-Collar Comedy Tour

HUMOR CAN BE AN ASSET AT THE OFFICE, BUT NOT FOR THE "FORWARDS FAIRY."

THE USE OF humor in the workplace can be a tremendous asset so long as your wit is quick and your selection of material is appropriate. Remember, everyone loves a good joke now and then, but everyone hates a bad joke, period. This chapter examines various types of office comedians, their material, deliveries, and what happens when they go overboard. My hope is that while reading these descriptions, you will be able to turn the spotlight inward and identify any warning signs that you might be pushing the levity limits around the office.

ROBIN WILLIAMS

Nobody does impressions like Robin Williams (though Darrell Hammond is right up there). The guy is a perfect mimic. He can completely transform himself by simply changing his facial expressions and altering the tone of his voice. I'm pretty confident claiming that nobody you work with can do voices like Robin Williams. Still, most offices have at least one Tool who tries.

I call him the "Routine Recycler." We all know this guy. He watches the same movies every weekend and memorizes all of the lines so that he can regurgitate them in the office all week. As I write this, his favorite impressions to butcher include *Borat* ("Sexy Time!") and a wide range of characters played by Will Ferrell. Oh ya, he probably also knows all the words to "Dick in a Box." He would have been all over Jim Carrey ("Somebody stop me!") in the '90s, and probably Chevy Chase ("Dr. Rosen-Rosen? Dr. Rosenpenis?") in the '80s.

The Routine Recycler often answers questions with quotes, followed by a self-affirming chuckle and the invitation to engage in a high five. Odds are good that he "could totally be on *Whose Line Is It Anyway?*" and has at least one epic idea for a TV pilot.

CHANDLER BING

There's always one amateur comedian who favors the sarcastic zingers made famous by Chandler Bing on *Friends*. The office Chandler will wait patiently in his cubicle until someone says something stupid, at which point he will shoot straight up (like the "whack-a-moles" at Chuck E. Cheese's) and say something snarky, to the effect of *"Riiiight, Jeanie. That plan makes perfect sense. Just let me call the president of Uganda and see if he can clear his schedule for lunch."*

Office Chandlers get obnoxious quickly. If you don't believe me, watch a few *Friends* reruns in a row on TBS. Part of the real Chandler's charm was that he only appeared for half an hour a week, and you could always turn him off when his shtick got old.

ROSE NYLUND

For those of you who missed both "Nick at Nite" and most of the '80s, Rose Nylund was the clueless and naïve *Golden Girl* played by Betty White. I contend that if Rose was working in an office today, she would be a "Forwards Fairy." No in-box is safe when the Forwards Fairy is on the loose. The Forwards Fairy is kind of like the Tooth Fairy, except that instead of leaving valuables under your pillow a few times a year, she leaves crap in your in-box every week.

The office Rose is generally much sweeter and more innocent than Robin Williams or Chandler Bing. She doesn't mean to be annoying, and probably doesn't have an idea that she is. Humor was never her game until she stumbled upon something funny on the Internet and realized that with just a click of the forward button she could share it with all her friends. Two hours and three really unfunny joke forwards later, she was addicted. Now she sends cute puppy pictures, chain e-mails, and YouTube clips to the entire list server on a daily basis.

JIM HALPERT

Jim Halpert is the office prankster on NBC's *The Office*. When Jim wants to be funny, people get Punk'd. Turn your back on Jim for one minute and you're likely to find your cell phone hidden in the ceiling rafters or your stapler encased in Jell-O mold. The real danger with Jim Halpert humor is that unlike Michael and Dwight on *The Office*, your colleagues are not likely to take pranks in stride. If you decide to become a prankster, you'd best be prepared to face some retaliation. Before you know it, your office will be a war zone. Paranoia will reign supreme, and productivity will take a swift nosedive. Eventually people will crack under the pressure. Better not leave coffee on your desk when you go to use the rest-room....

ANDY DICK

Ever seen Andy Dick do stand-up? Occasionally he's funny, but his material is always uncomfortable and inappropriate. He just goes way too far. Anyhow, there's bound to be a Dick or two in each office, cracking sex jokes and farting in the elevators. Make sure it isn't you or, like Andy Dick, you'll never make it off the B-list.

PAUL SHAFFER

Paul Shaffer, the musical director on *Late Night with David Letter-man*, is the ultimate sycophant, a total yes-man. No matter how pathetic Letterman's jokes are, Paul will reward him with a hearty belly laugh. He doesn't have a shred of comedic credibility. In fact, when you see Paul laugh on the show, it's a surefire sign that Dave has said something *unfunny*. He is no different from the Tool in your office who tries to win the boss's favor by laughing at every smarmy one-liner. He is particularly annoying because not only do his phony chuckles belong on a *Three's Company* laugh track, but his sucking up just inspires the boss to drop more awful jokes.

Now I'm no comedic expert. Furthermore, on any given day I am likely to dip into any one of the aforementioned profiles (most likely the Robin Williams). However, I do know one thing for certain: Humor is about your audience, and if they ain't feelin' it, you should stop dealin' it. Some people just don't like jokes. They don't like forwards, they don't like knock-knock jokes, and they particularly do NOT like Borat impressions. It's more important to read your audience than your material.

Little Habits of Horror

BEWARE OF RUDE LITTLE HABITS THAT MIGHT DRAW THE IRE OF STRESS MONSTERS AT THE OFFICE.

STRESS MONSTERS COME in all shapes and sizes. With deadlines approaching and work piled high, some people turn into werewolves, roaming the halls and howling all through the night. Others act more like zombies. They might move slowly and look dead, but they will rip your head off faster than you can say "flow chart." Then there are the gremlins, the night stalkers, the witches, and the ghosts, all of whom are equally deadly. It goes without saying that you shouldn't go out of your way to interrupt or provoke the stress monsters you encounter at the office. That means no barging into their offices and interrupting them when they are clearly busy or on the phone; no stopping them in the hall for idle chitchat when they are very obviously rushing into a meeting; or engaging in any other behavior that will be perceived as oblivious disregard for the value of their time and attention.

In addition, you also need to be aware of your annoying little habits, as they are just as likely as intentional interruptions to draw the ire of stress monsters. Do you know what I'm talking about?

Okay, think about some of the quirky habits you have that your boyfriend/girlfriend might find "cute." Maybe you're a fidgeter or you like to whistle off-key. Maybe you've got a "sweet wittle snif-fle," you bite your nails, or you can't go twenty minutes without rubbing smelly lotion all over your extremities. Though seemingly innocent, every one of these habits could attract the ire of a stress monster and get you killed.

In the interest of safety, I am going to list off a few specific habits and actions you should tone down at the office. In keeping with the theme of the chapter, I've lumped them into (hokey) horror movie–themed groups.

NIGHT OF THE LIVING DEAD

Stress zombies will not react well to friendly concern for their well-being. When you pass by a colleague who looks as though she hasn't slept in days and is obviously stressed out (dark eyes, wrinkled clothing, and kickin' breath are all telltale signs), do not say anything resembling the following:

> *"Wow, you look tired. You should probably go home and get some rest."*

or

> *"Are you sick? You look terrible!"*

or (God forbid)

> *"Too bad you've got to stay late. Well, now you know that you should just start earlier next time."*

In fact, don't offer comments about stress zombies' appearance at all. There's nothing more annoying than being told you look like crap in a cheerful and faux-friendly voice. I'm getting pissed off right now just thinking about it.

THE RING

Cell phones are always disruptive and annoying, particularly when people are stressed. Cutesy ringtones are downright infuriating. Ever been in a tense conference room when somebody's Austin Powers ringtone goes off? It ain't groovy, baby.

JAWS

Do you chew multiple pieces of gum at once? Do you chew with your mouth open? Do you smack your lips when you snack on chips? Do you talk with your mouth full? If so, watch out.

THE SIXTH SENSE

I can't even get my five basic senses functioning properly without coffee. If you were the one who finished off the last pot of coffee and didn't make a new one, or used the last filter and then neglected to open a new package, you'd better watch your back. You may not sense that anything is wrong, but I see dead people—and you're one of them.

TEXAS CHAINSAW MASSACRE

That's what I think of when I hear people coughing or clearing their throats all day long. You've got two choices: (1). Enter the Halls of Medicine, or (2) enter a world of pain.

SCREAM

Twenty-first-century phones are remarkably effective. They work so well, in fact, that there's really no need to scream into them when you are having a normal conversation. Your coworkers shouldn't hear you through the drywall. What's that? Your office doesn't even have full walls? Hmmm. You should probably step outside to take calls. It's for your own safety.

PART NINE

When the Going Gets Tough

LEARN TO NAVIGATE CONTROVERSY,
CONFRONTATIONS, AND DAYS THAT JUST
PLAIN SUCK.

Bad News and *The Bachelor*

DRAWING OUT THE DRAMA IS GREAT FOR TV BUT BAD FOR BUSINESS.

IF YOU WANT to learn how to deliver bad news professionally and with minimal fallout, watch any season finale of ABC's hit reality franchise *The Bachelor* and do the exact opposite of what you see. The show is a prime example of why good TV and good business are not one and the same. *The Bachelor*'s final "rose ceremony" provides some of the most dramatic moments on television, moments of unparalleled discomfort and anxiety that you would never want to experience at work.

For those of you who are not familiar with the show, the final rose ceremony is the climax of each season during which the Bachelor reveals to America whom he has chosen to become his companion for life (or at least the next few weeks). Twenty-five women begin each season vying for the Bachelor's affection, but only two survive the gauntlet of catfights, emotional breakdowns, group dates, and hometown visits required to make it to the final rose ceremony. Hopelessly in love, yet fully aware that her heart could be shattered before the end of the two-hour finale, each woman emerges from her limo dressed to the nines and worried as hell that she might not be the one to receive the Bachelor's final rose.

For the winner, the night will prove to be magical. For the loser, however, the evening will ultimately prove to be one of the most demoralizing of her life. And not because she'll have been turned down by the love of her life (or at least her love of the fall sweeps season) but because ABC wants the Bachelor to milk all the emotion out of the losing bachelorette before crushing her heart. Instead of having the decency to let the poor girl down quickly, the Bachelor draws it out until the last minute before he drops the bomb, and then promptly kicks her to the curb. Five minutes (and two Kleenex boxes) later in the limo, the loser will inevitably lose her mind and threaten to expose the Bachelor as a world-class scumbag. Wow. Not exactly the reaction you'd want from clients or coworkers, huh?

Here are a few suggestions for delivering bad news to help ensure you don't blow it like the Bachelor.

GET TO THE POINT.

When people are waiting on an important verdict, whether in court, business, or matters of the heart, they only care about one thing: yes or no. When an anxious bachelorette steps up to the Bachelor, she doesn't want to hear anything except whether or not she gets the damn rose. Still, the Bachelor always feels compelled to deliver the same "You're an amaaaazing person and I had an incredible time hiking in the mountains with you" speech before delivering his verdict. C'mon, dude. Get to the point already. Let the poor girl know the score before you drown her in verbal vomit.

Work is the same way. If you are asked to fire a coworker from a project or lose a supplier, don't begin with "Terry, you're an amaaaazing person. I'll always laugh when I remember the two of us at 3 a.m., locked out of that Comfort Inn in Tampa." Cut the crap and get down to business. Nobody pays attention to fluff when they are waiting on a verdict.

END ON A POSITIVE NOTE.

If the Bachelor were a smart guy, he would suck it up and begin with the heartbreak, *then* start gushing about what a wonderful person the losing bachelorette is. That way she would at least leave the house with a semisweet taste in her mouth, making her less likely to seek vengeance after the show wraps. It won't take the sting away, but at least he could rub on a little ointment to ease the pain. I suggest you do the same.

Again, let's say that you are asked to fire a supplier. Over the past year you have gotten to know that supplier's sales rep, Terry, pretty well. If the Bachelor were in your situation, he might say the following:

> *"Terry, you are one of the smartest people I've ever worked with in my career. . . ."* (At this point, Terry would feel all warm and fuzzy.) *"Unfortunately . . ."* (peace out, warm fuzzy)
> *". . . we can't keep buying product from your company. The numbers don't make sense for us. Hey, I've gotta run. Let's talk soon."*

The content of this message isn't that bad, but the chronology is bunk. When a compliment is immediately followed by bad news, the recipient experiences a dramatic emotional swing. On the other hand, if the bad news comes first, followed by the justification and the compliment, the emotional swing is more gradual and ends on a high note. Again, the message can stay consistent but you've got to flip the script:

"Terry, we can't keep buying product from your company. Unfortunately, the numbers don't make sense for us anymore. The decision has nothing to do with you, personally. In fact, I've enjoyed working with you a lot."

DON'T DANCE.

Up to this point we've been discussing how to deliver bad news in absolute love 'em or leave 'em situations. However, bad news is often required in smaller, less absolute doses. The problem is that people who aren't put on the spot and forced to state a go/no-go verdict will often try to dance around bad news. Dancing around bad news usually involves a slew of vague adjectives. For example, when someone from your office returns from a sales call and reports that they had a "useful" or "interesting" conversation, it means that they probably didn't sell anything. If they had, they would have said: "I sold X." Everyone knows that a vague adjective followed by a lengthy description of conversational minutiae is just an attempt to bore and/or confuse the audience into forgetting that nothing was actually accomplished.

Don't be a sissy. Own up when things go poorly so you can learn from your mistakes and/or develop a new strategy.

Delivering bad news is not easy. If it were, companies like World-Com wouldn't have spent years misstating their earnings to look better in front of their shareholders. Nobody likes to be a buzz kill, but you can't develop into a leader without learning to play the bad cop now and then.

Whoa, My Boss Is Naked!

DON'T BE AFRAID TO SPEAK UP IF YOU SPOT SOMETHING PECULIAR.

THE FOLLOWING IS a modern retelling of the classic fairy tale *The Emperor's New Clothes*.

Once upon a time in a faraway land there was a CEO who was obsessed with acquiring the most extravagant clothes. So addicted to suits, shoes, and French cuffs was he that his entire salary (plus bonuses) was directly deposited into retail outlets across the world.

One day two tailors entered the kingdom and declared that they had discovered the most elegant, beautiful, and expensive thread in the entire world. The thread was so luxurious, they claimed, that the only people who could see it were those elite few "worthy" of seeing it. The CEO was thrilled and immediately commissioned the tailors to fashion him a suit.

The tailors were given a lavish building in which to work and from time to time the CEO would send a couple low-level VPs to check up on them. Whenever the CEO's lieutenants en-

tered the workshop they would find the two tailors seated in
their ergonomic chairs, working hard at their sewing machines.
Now, given that there wasn't actually any thread to begin with,
the VPs would never actually see the clothes taking shape; however, they dared not admit it. Every senior staffer was well
aware that only those who were "worthy" of seeing the suit could
do so. Therefore every time a VP left the workshop, he/she would
return to the penthouse and give the CEO a glowing report of
how beautifully the suit was coming along.

After a few weeks, the tailors declared that the suit was finished and an "all hands on deck" meeting was scheduled to show
off the gorgeous garment. On the day of the meeting (which was
viewable via Webcast for the satellite offices) the CEO emerged
from his dressing room butt naked and beaming with pride. As
he stepped out onto the stage, the people cheered mightily yet
nervously (each distraught that he could not see the suit, yet unwilling to admit as much to his companions).

Right as the meeting was drawing to a close, an intern entered the auditorium, fresh from a trip to Starbucks. Upon catching a glimpse of the strutting streaker, he loudly exclaimed:
"Whoa, my boss is naked!" The intern's innocent observation
touched off a cacophony of murmurs throughout the crowd. The
murmurs turned to laughter as the people realized that the CEO
was, in fact, parading around naked.

Furious, the CEO had the tailors fired on the spot. Additionally, he realized the damaging extent of his vanity and toned
down his wardrobe from then on. Two weeks later, the intern
was promoted, the stock split, and they all lived happily ever
after.

Moral of the story: You are never too young or inexperienced to
speak up if you spot something amiss. In fact, your position as a relatively green "new kid" gives you a unique perspective from which

to pose provocative questions about the manner in which your organization is run. Your vantage point has not been tainted or obstructed by organizational cultures and courtesies, so if you come across something peculiar (maybe not as peculiar as someone strutting around in the buff... probably more like a set of numbers that doesn't make sense), do not assume that there is a good reason for it. Stand up and shout: "Hey, why is my boss naked?"

Make no mistake, asking questions takes courage, especially inquiries that could be viewed as "attacking" or "negative." But nobody is going to "off you" for questioning the establishment, so long as you do it in the right way.

When it comes to speaking up, keep the following points in mind:

RESPECT THE CHAIN OF COMMAND.

When you spot something peculiar, go to your immediate supervisor for clarification before taking your query up the food chain. More often than not, she/he will be able to provide context for your observations. It is neither appropriate nor productive for you to demand an audience with the CEO simply because you spotted a typo on the company Web site. Which brings us to the next point...

PICK AND CHOOSE YOUR *ERIN BROCKOVICH* MOMENTS.

Don't be a whistle-blower for the sake of making a name for yourself. That's what Corporate Tools do and it's annoying as hell. Focus your energy on finding answers to problems, not creating controversy for the sake of a little airtime.

Don't Hate the Player, Hate the Game

YOU CAN'T FAULT COWORKERS FOR ACCEPTING REWARDS YOU BELIEVE TO BE UNJUSTIFIED.

ON FEBRUARY 11, 2002, the Canadians got hosed. After delivering a near flawless performance and winning over the hearts of viewers across the world, Olympic darlings Jamie Salé and David Pelletier stared in disbelief as their hard-earned pairs figure skating gold medals were awarded to the Russians. Not to take anything away from Berezhnaya and Sikharulidze (the Russian duo), because they had performed well, but c'mon ... they botched a double axel, for the love! It was robbery, I tell you! Robbery, eh!

At that moment, millions of well-mannered, even-keeled Canadians collectively lost it, hurling empty cans of Labatt Blue at their television sets while shouting obscenities at the French judge (who bore a striking resemblance to Cruella De Vil from Disney's *101 Dalmatians*). Salé and Pelletier, on the other hand, kept their composure and respectfully congratulated the Russian tandem. Even though the judges had obviously screwed them over, they elected to take the high road.

As it turned out, the International Olympic Committee discovered that unethical collusion had, in fact, taken place between Cruella De Vil and the Russian judge, so they awarded a second set of gold medals to Salé and Pelletier, vaulting the pair into the brightest fifteen minutes of fame they could have ever hoped to achieve.

In business, as in figure skating, everyone performs a unique routine with loose criteria that is evaluated subjectively by one or more judges. Unfortunately, errors in judgment occur more frequently in the working world than the skating world. Countless slacker employees are unjustly promoted or rewarded every day over their more deserving peers. When you are on the short end of a shady judgment at work it can be demoralizing and infuriating. You can't help but resent others for accepting the recognition you believe you have earned. However, before acting on such frustration, take a step back and consider the teachings of one Snoop Dogg: "Don't hate the player, hate the game." That is, there is no point in faulting coworkers for being successful. Even if you feel an injustice has occurred, the blame should be directed at the people, organization, or industry that would allow them to get ahead.

If you work hard and perform well, you'll get yours, rest assured. Don't sour your chances by throwing a tantrum and alienating your peers.

Produce Exhibit A

PROTECT YOUR WORK AND YOUR BACKSIDE BY DOCUMENTING IMPORTANT COMMUNICATIONS.

EVER WORKED WITH an "I got screwed" guy? The guy who is always ranting and raving about how the world and everyone in it is out to get him? C'mon, you know who I'm talking about. He blames every unfavorable outcome on some malevolent force outside his control—computer problems when reports are past due, car accidents or random emergencies every time he's late, the wind for every missed putt, and so forth. Odds are good that he hasn't made it past middle manager because "BS politics" caused him to get passed over for several promotions. For the "I got screwed" guy, it is inconceivable to suggest that laziness and lack of work ethic directly correlate with his failure to perform.

Unfortunately, most offices have an "I got screwed" guy and maybe even an "I got screwed" gal to boot. When the tide is high, you'd never suspect trouble from them because they are usually the ones down to joke around and hang out at the office. After all, goofing off is more fun than actually working, right? On the other hand, when the milk starts to go sour, you'd better be prepared. "I got screwed" folks get defensive awful quick and try to deflect external scrutiny by loudly placing blame on anyone and anything within arm's reach. So, if you happen to sit at the desk next door . . . watch your back.

You want to avoid getting screwed by the "I got screwed" crew? Well then you'd better start documenting. Your achievements, failures, communications, and goals should be captured on paper, or at least in your e-mail archive. When the shit hits the fan and the blame starts flying, you don't want to be sent to the guillotine because you couldn't produce written exhibits that were admissible in court.

YOU MUST PROTECT THIS HOUSE!

In addition to leaving yourself vulnerable to the "I got screwed" crew, failure to properly document important communications will leave your work vulnerable to poachers. If you delete the e-mail about your great new idea, or misplace that report outlining the contributions you made on that last project, you could lose credit faster than Mark McGwire after a steroids hearing.

Here's a hypothetical: Imagine that you are a young radio astronomer who has spent the last several years wasting away in the New Mexico desert, searching for signs of extraterrestrial life. You have sacrificed everything for your work, including money and career stability. It goes without saying that you have no social life. Anyhow, several years into the project you finally hear something on one of your machines. It's gotta be aliens. Yes! They are telling you to build a one-person machine that will allow you to communicate with them. This is unreal!

Naturally, as the foremost alien communications expert in the country, you will be the person selected to man the machine. That is, unless your golden ticket gets swiped by the dude who played Viper in *Top Gun*.

I am, of course, rehashing the plotline from the film *Contact*, in which Dr. Ellie Arroway (Jodie Foster) makes an inexcusable career mistake by entrusting all of her scientific secrets and methods to her colleague, David Drumlin (Tom Skerritt), who promptly uses them to further his own career at her expense. By the time Ellie realizes what's going on, she is powerless to stop Drumlin because she failed to document any of their prior conversations. All of Drumlin's implied promises and verbal assurances weren't worth the bad breath they flew in on.

SPOILER ALERT. If you haven't seen this movie, and (for whatever reason) plan to rent it someday, skip the next paragraph.

Now as luck would have it, Drumlin gets blown up by a sectarian terrorist before the machine is activated and Ellie ends up getting to meet the aliens anyway.* But that doesn't mean I'm going to let dear Dr. Arroway off the hook. She wouldn't have needed to be saved by an extremist intervention had she just protected herself with documentation in the first place.

---

*Hey, it's the movies. Crazy things happen. Actually, the craziest thing about *Contact* for me was that Matthew McConaughey was cast as a priest. That's less believable than the aliens.

TODAY, DOCUMENTING IS EASY LIKE SUNDAY MORNING.

E-mail makes it easy to protect yourself from the "I got screwed" crew and protect your work from poaching coworkers. If you feel as though a colleague is acting shady, just shoot them a question-based e-mail. For example, if you are addressing an "I got screwed" guy who isn't pulling his weight you could send the following:

"Steve, missed you at the brainstorming meeting last night. Is everything okay?"

Even if Steve doesn't answer the e-mail, your server will memorialize the message. Thus Steve will be much less likely to throw you under the bus if the project doesn't go well, because he knows you know he slacked off–and that you have the e-mail to prove it.

Meanwhile, if you are sending a "credit protection" message to a coworker, it could say:

"Shelly, I'm glad you enjoyed reading my research on xyz. When do you think we should make Janet aware of the findings?"

Do you know how difficult it was to memorialize this type of information twenty years ago? You probably would have had to wear a wire like Big Pussy on *The Sopranos* to get the same effect ... and look what happened to him (he now sleeps with the fishes). Actually, forget that last part. The wire parallel suggests that you are out to trap your colleagues, when in fact you are just taking out theft insurance.

Put Some Space Between Yourself and the Office

A PROACTIVE COMMUNICATION STRATEGY CAN LAND YOU ON THE WEEKEND "DO NOT CALL" LIST.

I N T H E 1999 classic *Office Space*, an unending cycle of last-minute weekend work drives the main character, Peter, to commit criminal acts. Peter finally snaps one Friday afternoon after his douche bag boss, Lumbergh, kills yet another weekend by showing up at Peter's cubicle and asking him to come in the next day. Long story short, Peter ends up conspiring with two equally frustrated colleagues to steal vast amounts of money from their employer, Initech. Naturally, hijinks ensue. In the end, only a well-timed explosion set off by an equally disenchanted employee keeps Peter and his friends from getting busted.

Unlike Peter, you need to address your frustrations regarding after-hours assignments before criminal plots creep into your mind. If you feel as though your name is disproportionately called when there is weekend work to be done, you should consider taking the following preventative measures:

BE DIRECT.

If you feel like you're getting a raw deal and there doesn't seem to be any reason or reward to justify the extra work, direct communication with your boss is the best remedy. That said, you'd better do some homework and confirm your suspicions before airing your grievances. If it turns out that all your peers are getting just as much extra work as you are, bitching won't help matters at all. In fact, you will probably be rewarded with even more work to go along with your new reputation as a "whiny punk."

TRY THE TIME-STAMP APPROACH.

If your boss is unreasonable or unapproachable (or just a clueless Tool like Lumbergh) and direct communication isn't an option, there are several effective indirect methods you can deploy. For example, make sure to e-mail your boss or work group when you burn the midnight oil. Summarize the project you are working on, pose a question to the group, and so forth. To be honest, the subject matter isn't critical. The time stamp is what you're playing for. Once your boss notices that you are sending work e-mails at 2 a.m. he/she will be less likely to call your name for the graveyard shift in the future. At the very least, you'll have documentation of all the extra time you put in to help you build your case when asking for your next raise or promotion.

VOLUNTEER YOUR SERVICES AHEAD OF TIME.

Another tactic you can employ to get your name added to the weekend "do not call" list is to proactively volunteer your services ahead of time. More specifically, you can volunteer for extracurricular tasks that jibe with your schedule. While it may still suck to work on the weekend, it will suck far less if you can plan the extra work around your life. Moreover, you will undoubtedly score bonus points for being a "self-starter" and "team player."

When my wife, Sarah, was in college, she spent a summer working in a lab at a hospital in suburban Chicago. The lab was running several experiments with live cells, and one of Sarah's bosses had been saddled with the assignment of coming in on Saturdays to feed the cells in order to ensure that the cells would survive the weekend and remain useful for experiments the following week. Unfortunately, the woman lived forty minutes away in downtown Chicago. Sarah, on the other hand, lived less than a mile from the lab. Recognizing that the hour she'd lose out of her weekend paled in comparison to the three-hour loss suffered by her boss, Sarah volunteered to go in and feed the cells. Not only was Sarah never called upon to do any other night/weekend activities, but her grateful boss wrote her a killer recommendation for medical school.

When you are a junior-level employee, impromptu after-hours projects are part of the game. You should take them in stride and complete them thoroughly. That said, if you feel your free time (and good nature) is being unfairly exploited, speak up. There's nothing wrong with taking steps to protect your weekend.

The Strength to Carrey On

HOW BAD WAS YOUR DAY, REALLY?

SHIT HAPPENS. YOU'RE going to have bad days now and then. When bad days strike, it is important to consider the following question before reacting: *How bad was my day, really?* Was it a "not enough sleep, boss yelled at me, and Panera ran out of chicken and wild rice" day, or a "my car was totaled, my boyfriend is cheating, and I was wrongly accused of stealing from the company" day? When it comes to dealing with bad days at work, perspective is paramount. Not all bad days were created equal.

The chart that follows examines three Jim Carrey characters that had bad day debacles at work—and what you can learn from them.

CHARACTER NAME/MOVIE	Stanley Ipkiss/ *The Mask* (1994)	Bruce Nolan/ *Bruce Almighty* (2003)	Truman Burbank/ *The Truman Show* (1998)
Occupation	Bank clerk	News reporter	Insurance agent
Biggest gripe at work	Feels stuck in low-level monotony	Feels as though his talent is never recognized	Feels like he has no control over his career
Actual problem	He is a pushover who allows others to walk all over him.	He is self-absorbed and has an inflated sense of entitlement.	He has no control over his life, as he is (unknowingly) starring in a reality TV program.
Bad day overview	Jerk boss yells at him, colleagues take advantage of his generous personality, and his friends ditch him later in the evening.	Bruce gets sent to do a demeaning assignment and then discovers he has been passed over for a desired promotion at work.	Truman discovers that his entire life and career have been staged. He realizes that he has never truly earned or accomplished anything.
Reaction	With the aid of a magical mask, he robs the bank at which he works and then paints the town in style by throwing money around and picking fights.	He throws a tantrum and hurls insults at his boss and coworkers while on the air, subsequently gets fired, and later picks an ill-advised fight with a street gang (he loses badly).	He nearly loses his mind and then decides to walk off the set of his faux-life.
Wakes up the next day and feels . . .	Mortified	Defeated	Liberated
Lessons learned	You need to stand up for yourself *before* you allow repressed frustrations to boil over.*	Don't react drastically while you are still emotionally charged.	If everything looks, feels, and smells wrong, get the hell out.

*The central story line of *The Mask* bears an uncanny resemblance to *Me, Myself, and Irene* (2000), another Carrey movie. In each film a timid lead character (played by Carrey) gets pushed around one time too many and retaliates via a brash alter ego. In *Irene*, Carrey develops an evil, mischievous second personality that takes control of his life in much the same fashion as Ipkiss's mask. As such, please feel free to substitute *Irene* for *Mask* when reading this chart if it makes you more comfortable.

Of the three characters chronicled in the chart, only Truman's bad day was truly worthy of a drastic reaction. The other two characters let their emotions get the better of them and overreacted, which put their careers (and their lives) in serious jeopardy.

If you're having a bad day, try not to make any rash decisions or take drastic action while you're still angry or emotionally charged. Instead, take a walk, eat a nice dinner, chill with your friends, cozy up to your Wii, whatever. Let the experience marinate for a day before you start cookin'. If you wake up in the morning after a bad day and the veins are still poppin', then you should probably go talk to someone about it. Whatever you do, don't throw an almighty tantrum like Bruce Nolan or mask your frustration with aggression like Stanley Ipkiss did. It will only turn your bad day into a worse week.

PART TEN

Out of the Chat Room, Into the Board Room

MySpace Is Everyone's Space

WHO NEEDS BACKGROUND CHECKS WHEN YOU'VE GOT THE INTERNET?

ONE OF MY younger brother's MySpace friends is apparently also friends with several hookers. Okay, okay, I don't know that they're hookers, for sure. They could be exotic dancers. I know for a fact that at least one is a porn star because I've seen her life story chronicled on VH1. No matter.

In addition to hanging out with hookers/strippers/porn stars, my brother's friend also seems to spend a lot of time admiring his car, drinking 40s, flexing his pecs, and referring to himself in the third person. Did I mention he makes great Zoolander faces? Rumor has it he's looking for a job right now...

MySpace is public space, people. There's nothing private about it. If you want to store naked pictures from spring breaks past, buy a photo album. As soon as you post stuff on the Internet, it's fair game for the rest of the world. Remember the twenty-six-year-old high school art teacher from Texas who posted some "artistic" pictures of herself on MySpace? She got canned as soon as they were discovered (although attendance in her classes went way up). Go figure.

Think before you post! The Internet is a voyeuristic place, and HR is watching. If you're active on MySpace, Facebook, and/or any other social networking sites, monitor your pages closely. The last thing you need is an e-mail from your boss with the heading "About your Amsterdam trip..."

Proof Reed You're Emales

ANYTHING WORTH WRITING IS WORTH EDITING.

A COUPLE YEARS AGO I got the green light to hire my first college intern. I probably spent three hours writing and editing a one-page job posting and then sent it on to two colleagues for proofreading before submitting it to employment Web sites. The next morning I had four new e-mails with attached résumés from eager applicants. I opened the first one. It read something like this:

Dear Mr. Green, my name is @#$%^@# and I am very interested in an internship with your company. Please find my résumé and cover letter attached.

Guess what? I didn't even waste time looking for his résumé. My last name is Greene, with an *e* on the end. In my mind, the candidate couldn't possibly have been that interested in working for me if he didn't even take the time to spell my name correctly. His résumé and cover letter may have shown him to be the most qualified candidate I could have ever hoped for, but I didn't even read them. Sound fickle? Perhaps, but what message does it send to a potential employer about your ability to attend to details when you don't even take the time to spell his/her name correctly?

In the electronic age, your e-mails are every bit as important as formal documents, presentations, and cover letters. More and more, e-mails are serving as first impressions for clients, colleagues, and employers. Therefore they should be taken seriously and edited meticulously. Don't treat e-mail like voice mail—that is, as an improvised greeting. With e-mail, everything you say is "on the record." Whether you're sending progress reports to clients or simply responding to a lunch invitation from the dude in the cubicle down the hall, make sure that you check over all of your written communications. Think about your goal for each message before you type, while you're typing, and after you type. Consider your relationship with your intended target and make sure to use an appropriate level of formality and tone. In other words, don't start an e-mail to the CFO with "Hey Bill, what's shaking," unless the two of you are family or former roommates. On the flip side, there's no need to address your lunch buddies with excessive formality. I hate it when my friends send me e-mails with formal closings, like "Warmest regards" or "Sincerely." So lame.

Are you initiating a conversation or responding to a previous e-mail? If the latter is true, you should check over the previous thread to ensure that you've answered all outstanding questions. Speaking from experience, it is infuriating when somebody waits a day or two to respond to an e-mail and then ignores your initial questions completely. That's bush league.

Finally (and this goes for documents as well as e-mails) USING SPELL CHECK IS NOT THE SAME AS EDITING. Contrary to what one of my former roommates used to believe, Spell Check is not writer's Tylenol.* You can't just run Spell Check and assume that it will make all of your boo-boos go away. If you are in a bad state, Spell Check won't even numb the pain. Worse, you could end up with sentences that look like this:

Know I don't get it. Why wood Mr. Brewster put Cathy in that roll?

It is absolutely necessary to edit and proofread all of your work e-mails. Anything worth writing is worth editing.

---

*It's worth noting that the same roommate considered incense to be the Tylenol of air fresheners.

E-mail Responses: All for One or One for All?

E-MAIL RESPONSES, FIRE ALARMS, AND THE "NEED TO KNOW" BASIS

CORPORATE TOOLS POUND the "reply all" button like it's
Natty Light at a ten-year reunion. In my opinion, "reply all"
should be treated like a fire alarm. If you're going to go out
of your way to grab everyone's attention, something had better be
burning up. Remember what happened to kids who pulled the fire
alarm on a whim in school? They got sent home faster than Steve
Urkel on a first date. I think the same thing should happen to people who abuse the "reply all" button on work e-mails. Same goes
for the jerks who attach the red "urgent/high importance" symbol
to every inane e-mail they send out. If you can't discern what is or
isn't important enough to warrant mass disruption, you should get
a one-way ticket back to your apartment to think it over.

When you send unwarranted "reply all" or "high importance"
messages at work, it's like you are spamming your coworkers. The
only real difference is that most spammers use aliases so that
pissed off recipients don't know where to find them. You, on the
other hand . . .

The following are some of the worst reply-all tactics:

NOT-SO-SUBTLE SELF-PROMOTION

9:04 a.m. The boss sends an e-mail to your entire department congratulating you all on a project well done.

9:10 a.m. The brownnoser at the desk next to you uses the "reply all" button and sends the following message: *Thanks, Terri. I worked nonstop on those graphics for three days. I should probably reintroduce myself to my family after work tonight!–JB.*

How annoying is that? What on earth would prompt someone to share his/her sucking up with the group? Furthermore, what kind of douche bag goes out of his/her way to extract individual accolades from group glory? Not-so-subtle self-promotional responses reek of insecurity and Toolishness.

THE LAST WORD

It has been my experience that the "reply all" button is most frequently abused when coworkers feel their honor is at stake. In other words, during useless e-Arguments. E-Arguments usually spring up when things aren't going so hot. You lose a little business, somebody sends out an admonishing e-mail, and then all of a sudden an online riot breaks out. Pretty soon your e-mail box is flooded with transcribed catfights. The only people who really pay attention to the threads are the combatants themselves, yet they feel as though they need to save face by getting the last word in in front of the whole group. Problem is, unlike face-to-face arguments, e-Arguments can carry on for an indefinite amount of time if the parties involved are stubborn enough.

If you have a beef with someone at the office, limit your e-Argument correspondence to the people directly involved. And whatever you do, do NOT try to settle an e-Argument by adding someone's boss or supervisor onto the e-mail for the sole purpose of getting that person in trouble. Whether or not the person is to blame is irrelevant. Nobody likes a narc.

ONE-LINE WISECRACK

The most pointless "high-importance reply all" e-mail is the one-line wisecrack. Contrary to what you might think, the worst one-liners aren't of the chillingly unfunny variety. In fact, the lame-liners are fairly harmless. The clever comments are the ones that piss me off. Why? Because a clever one-liner can trigger a barrage of less clever follow-up quips from slightly amused coworkers who now feel compelled to prove that they can be equally witty. Once the one-liners start flying, the entire thread is rendered worthless because no one is going to sift through the one-liner pollution in search of a relevant or useful posting.

When it comes to the "reply all" and "urgent/high importance" buttons, please exercise restraint. If you consistently abuse (and then lose) your e-mail credibility, coworkers will just toss your unopened messages into the trash alongside spam offers for generic Canadian Viagra.

LOL = Loser Online

"EBBREVIATIONS" BELONG IN JUNIOR HIGH, NOT AT THE OFFICE.

ELECTRONIC ABBREVIATIONS ("*e*BBREVIATIONS") are unprofessional, extremely Toolish, and should be banished from all your work correspondence. Eighth grade is over, so take your headphones off, put down the Mountain Dew, and show your colleagues the courtesy of typing out entire words.

Among the obnoxious ebbreviations, LOL (Laughing Out Loud) is undoubtedly the worst. I will concede that LOL was cute when it first came out and I abused it as much as the next kid. However, at that time I was also wearing my dad's XXL flannel shirts and listening to Boyz II Men. I guess what I'm saying is that LOL has no place in the twenty-first century. And like flannel shirts and "Motownphilly," it has no place in the office, either.

The LOL of today bears no resemblance to the genuine expression of joy it represented when the Internet was young. For an adult, LOL can mean a number of things ranging from "the forward you just sent me was vaguely amusing" to "I need an excuse to get your boring ass to stop sending me messages so I can buy shoes online, or focus on my fantasy football draft." Either way, LOL is just something people type when they have nothing of substance to communicate. When you are in the early stages of your career, the last thing you want is to be known as a person who doesn't have anything useful to say.

Though some ebbreviations are more functional and genuine than LOL, using them in a business setting is just as immature and unprofessional. Can you imagine Donald Trump ever typing ebbreviations at work? Check this out:

> Tracy–
> ATM, I am very disappointed with the status of our quarterly earnings. Over the past couple of months, you have made several inexcusable oversights . . .
> (BRB)
> . . . which have resulted in millions of dollars in lost revenue. IMHO, such mismanagement is unacceptable and I have no choice but to let you go.
> FYI, you're fired.
>
> > TTYL,
> > The Donald

While I'm venting, I might as well add that it's even worse when people use ebbreviation "sequels." For example, when I was brainstorming ideas for this chapter, I asked my dad about the ebbreviations he'd seen used at his law firm. He's not exactly Mr. Wizard on the computer, so I figured he'd just answer with the basics. Instead, the first thing to come out of his mouth was the LOL follow-up "ROFL"–rolling on the floor laughing. ROFL is the worst sequel since "*too fast, too furious.*" But my dad assumed ROFL was a "hip" phrase to use in casual communication with younger colleagues. Meanwhile, when he said it I wanted to "ROFSMR"– *roll on the floor and stab myself repeatedly.*

All of your written communications at work should be professional, period. If I had my way, people who used ebbreviations at the office would be suspended or assigned to work on the yearbook.

I Might Shoot the Messenger

IT'S TIME TO ESTABLISH SOME GROUND RULES FOR SENDING INSTANT MESSAGES AT WORK.

BUILDING ON THE thread from the last chapter, I'd like to take a moment to discuss instant messages. As IMs become a bigger part of daily business communication, I think it's important to establish some ground rules. Here's my take.

1. **Turn off your volume**. This is pretty basic. Nobody wants to hear your IM message noises chiming nonstop throughout the day.
2. **Erase the smiley faces**. To me, adults who send smiley face "emoticons" over instant messenger are the same people who wear Disney character sweatshirts and proudly display sets of commemorative plates bought directly from TV.
3. **Limit multi-typing**. Don't be an instant messenger whore, that is, the guy/girl who types to eight people at once. If your desktop is so full of instant message boxes that it resembles the board from *Hollywood Squares* (sans Whoopi Goldberg and Jim J. Bullock), I'm calling you out.

4. **Thou shalt refrain from using IM during boring meetings and/or conference calls.** I have a buddy, Ken, who used to work with me. He and I were in a boring meeting one day, listening to an utter moron give an utterly moronic talk. Anyhow, Ken decided it would be funny to send me an instant message containing a harsh evaluation of the speaker. Unfortunately, Ken failed to notice that my laptop was hooked up to the LCD projector at the front of the room. When Ken pushed send, the message "Don't make me work with this idiot" appeared on the big screen for the whole meeting to see. It's not easy to talk your way out of a situation like that.

5. **If the content is important, pick up the phone.** I don't care how much of a computer whiz you think you are, nobody can deliver information as accurately, or convey a range of emotions as fully by typing as he/she can by phone or in person . . . with the possible exception of Stephen Hawking.

6. **Don't send legally sensitive information over IM.** I really hope you don't need me to explain myself on this one. If the subject of your message concerns hiring, firing, or the secret sauce, keep it off the desktop.

Screw You Guys, I'm Going Virtual

DON'T LET THE E-WORLD TAKE OVER THE REAL WORLD.

SOUTH PARK MIGHT be the funniest show on television. Though I find it extremely tough to pick and choose between episodes, I'd have to say my favorite is "Make Love, Not Warcraft." In that episode, the boys become obsessed with the online role-playing game "World of Warcraft." They spend so much time developing their virtual characters (Cartman is a dwarf, Stan is a Knight, etc.) that they begin to lose touch with the real world. Over the next couple weeks, they refuse to leave their computer chairs. Cartman even installs an intercom so he can call upstairs for Hot Pockets. As a result, all four kids double in size, get hooked on energy drinks, and develop some kickin' acne.

The episode provides a hilarious reminder of what can happen when virtual world personalities overtake real-world lives. We all spend countless hours working on the computer each day, so who's to say that we haven't developed our own little virtual-executive personalities. Think about it: Maybe your virtual-executive personality is like a Troll (blunt, pugnacious, and impatient). Or perhaps you're more like a Wizard (sly, preachy, and patronizing) or a Warrior

Princess (sweet and innocent, yet deadly when provoked). Whatever character you assume when you saddle up in your Office Max throne, you should be aware that your virtual personality has a real-world effect on your life and your career.

Computer battles happen as often in the office as they do in the basement. Chippy e-mails, stolen credit or ideas, and/or critiques of honor can all incite virtual combat. Unlike "World of Warcraft," however, you can't just turn off the game when the carnage ends and resume your old identity. If "virtual you" is a jerk on Monday, your real-life peers will be pissed on Tuesday.

CH. 50

Don't Get Locked in Solitaire Confinement

THERE'S NO SUCH THING AS "JUST ONE GAME."

THIS IS YOUR career:

This is your career on Solitaire:

I firmly believe that the "Microsoft Games" package kills more time and brain cells than marijuana, and is just as addictive as crack. Solitaire (Spider or regular), FreeCell, Minesweeper, Reversi, Hearts–they're all just drugs, boys and girls. Don't laugh at the comparison because I'm dead serious. If you get hooked, your work will suffer, your colleagues will notice, and pretty soon you'll be eating a steady diet of government cheese and living in a van down by the river.

Online games are sneaky little drugs. You never realize you're addicted because you don't suffer from the same symptoms as normal junkies. No scratching at imaginary insects, no fevers, and no bankruptcy (since the game is given out for free by the pushers at Microsoft). But once you sit down at the computer, the games call to you with the irresistible siren song of the last donut hole.

> *"Hey, Jennifer, how's about taking a quick Minesweeper break?"*
>
> *"No way,"* you tell yourself. *"I've got a meeting in two hours and a project due tomorrow."*
>
> *"C'mon,"* the games say. *"Just one game. You almost beat the four-suit spider yesterday ..."*
>
> *"Okay, but just one game."*

Just like that, you're screwed. As I write this, I've got FreeCell open in another window. I should have been done with this chapter two days ago, but the ace of clubs was buried in the top row ...

The craziest thing is that these games aren't even fun! But when you are stuck at work, they are, as Dave Matthews would say, the best of what's around. Solitaire is to the office what paper football and origami fortune-telling were to elementary school. And a quick fix is just a click away.

Unfortunately, I have yet to stumble across a suitable MS games detox program. Therefore, you're on your own in kicking the habit. Stay strong. Mind over Minesweeper. Don't cave in to your Solitaire-y urges. Do not play them before lunch. Do not play them after lunch. Do not play them on your break. Do not play them with some cake. Do not play them now and then. Do not play them ever again! Free your mind from FreeCell and get back to work.

PART ELEVEN

Get a Life (Preferably Your Own)

A FEW THOUGHTS ON THE IMPORTANCE OF CHILLING OUT, AND THE HORRORS OF "TOOLS GONE WILD"

Bruce Wayne vs. Clark Kent

ALL ALTER EGOS ARE NOT CREATED EQUAL.

EVERY DECENT SUPERHERO has an alter ego, a distinctly separate identity that is assumed when he/she gets off work. Possessing such an identity has a number of benefits for superheroes, not the least of which is privacy. Alter ego identities are kept secret from employers, customers, and coworkers, allowing superheroes to walk casually among the general population without being hassled.

In theory, the adoption of alter egos should allow all superheroes to separate their work selves from their real selves and to unwind and de-stress without nagging worries about yet to be completed projects. In practice, however, this is not always the case. Like the mainstream working population, some superheroes are able to remove themselves from work-related stress through leisure activities and relaxation, while others can't seem to get a life. I've sketched out a quick comparison between (arguably) the two most famous alter egos around, Clark Kent (Superman) and Bruce Wayne (Batman), to illuminate the disparity.

Alter Ego	Clark Kent	Bruce Wayne
What he's like outside of work	*Awkward, stressed*	*Calm, cool, and collected*
His hobbies outside of work	*Thinking about work, stalking Lois*	*Throwing parties, collecting art*
Methods for relaxing at home	*Not sure he ever goes home*	*Glass of wine and a good book by the fireplace*
Policy re: working late	*Constantly thinking about work and looking for more to do*	*Willing to help out if the office calls (signals in the sky)*
Close friends or confidants	*None*	*Alfred, Dick Grayson (Robin's alter ego)*

Right now you might be wondering the following: *If Superman was so maladjusted and unhealthy, how come he is the most successful and revered hero of modern times?* After all, Superman is the gold standard. If he doesn't need to chill out and have a life outside of work, why do the rest of us? Well, to put it bluntly, the guy's not human. He is not of our planet. If Superman were human, he'd be on track for a heart attack before his fortieth birthday, no questions asked. Think about it. The dude is always stressed.

If Clark Kent worked in Corporate America, I'm pretty sure he would join his company's "work/life balance" committee. He'd try to make himself feel better about lacking a life outside the office by putting a "Work to live, don't live to work" sticker on his cubicle wall. He'd fill out a work/life worksheet every week to prove that he was engaging in healthy activities outside the office. Unfortunately, getting a life isn't about filling out scorecards or branding your extracurricular attitude. You shouldn't need to attend a corporate training session in order to learn how to get a life. You just need to commit to removing yourself from the stresses of the office every now and then, so you don't develop into the dickhead who instinctively checks work e-mail in between innings of his kids' little league games. Seriously, that guy sucks.

Bruce Wayne, on the other hand, has a life outside his work. He is relaxed, human, and knows how to chill. Earlier in this book I mentioned that many Corporate Tools currently go out of their way to mimic Batman. Unfortunately, they emulate the wrong things. Hot cars and beltline gadgets don't make Batman the hero he is. Batman is calm, cool, and collected under fire. He isn't overly stressed, because he's comfortable with who he is, whether he's on call or kickin' it in the cave. He knows that there is a time to kick ass and a time to kick back. He is super at both.

Models and Bottles

"LEISURE BINGING" IS A DESPERATE AND DANGEROUS GAME.

THERE'S NOTHING QUITE like spending forty-eight hours in Vegas. I love it. I love the hotels, the food, the casinos, and the people watching. I love how the atmosphere on a Vegas-bound flight rivals that of the bus to summer camp. I love asking for eight keys to my hotel room and not catching any crap for it. I love starting out the night playing $25 blackjack at the Bellagio and finishing the night throwing $2 craps at O'Shea's.* I love getting more sleep by the pool than I do in my bed. I think you get the picture.

Unfortunately, the Vegas potion wears off after a couple days and when it does, I begin to notice things. Sad things. I notice the garbage, the hookers, the headaches, and the little kids who have just realized that Daddy was lying when he said Vegas was "just

---

*O'Shea's is one of the only casinos on the strip that still has $2 craps. The drinks are watery and the place smells like a used shoebox with a cigarette in it, but if you're up for rolling $2 dice at 4 a.m. in Vegas you probably won't mind.

like Disneyland." More than anything else, however, I start notic-ing desperation all over the place. Hour forty-nine is when I no-tice all the people who are trying to "get it all back" with one roll. They're exhausted, sweaty, and down to their last black chip. It's 8 a.m., yet they're still leaning over the roulette table, screaming at the wheel in between sips of a half-empty Jack and Coke. They know in their hearts that there's no way they can recoup the ten grand they lost over the weekend, but they're gonna go down swinging and swigging. I told you, it's pretty sad.

I bring this up because the "get it all back" mentality of the forty-ninth-hour Vegas gambler is very similar to the social men-tality of the workaholic Corporate Tool. Corporate Tools who don't make time for a life outside the office are prone to "leisure binging" when they do go out. For some reason, they believe that if they throw money around and party like D-list celebrities one Saturday a month, they will make up for all the social time lost while they were pulling all-nighters and polishing off TPS reports. Unfortunately, they reek of desperation.

Here are a few more reasons why leisure binging will never be an adequate substitute for getting a life:

LEISURE BINGING IS TOO STRESSFUL.

In *American Psycho*, leisure binging is a competitive sport for Patrick Bateman and his Corporate Tool buddies. They don't really enjoy going out; they just enjoy creating the perception that they had the best time. Fun becomes stressful because they feel pressure to have the ultimate top-shelf experience: the best food, the most beautiful people, and the hottest clubs. Anything less and they feel like their fun was second best. Consider this Bateman quote: "As we arrive at Espace I'm on the verge of tears as I'm certain we won't get a decent table. But we do. Relief washes over me in an awesome wave."

Leisure time shouldn't be stressful; it should be enjoyable and relaxing, and in no way resemble any scene from *American Psycho*.

LEISURE BINGING IS UNHEALTHY.

If you feel bad that you haven't made time for your beer buddies all month, don't compensate by drinking a whole case of High Life in one shot. You won't remember the evening fondly if you end up getting your stomach pumped. Like pyramid schemes or diet pills ("Trim Spa, Baaaby"), leisure binging is just an empty shortcut. For every person who claims it works, there are a hundred unsatisfied customers. Leisure binging is unhealthy and will just make you feel worse about yourself.

LEISURE BINGING IS TRANSPARENTLY TOOLISH.

Let's head back to Vegas for a moment. In Vegas, leisure bingers are easier to spot than working girls at the hotel bar. My buddy Matt, a bartender who has spent a lot of time in Sin City, says the transparency is due to the phony, choreographed celebrating that Tools do when they are out on the town.

"They're like showboats dancing in an NFL end zone," says Matt. "If they were true professionals, they would act like they'd been there before."

It's ironic that the process of trying to look as cool as possible is what makes Corporate Tools look like even bigger losers. It's sad, really. As I told you earlier, I've seen a lot of sad things in Vegas.

Avoid Becoming *Mean Girls* and Wise Guys

THE SLIPPERY SLOPE FROM UNDERCOVER TO UNDER THE INFLUENCE

NOBODY WAKES UP one day and decides to become a workaholic Corporate Tool. It just kind of happens over time. One minute you're a bright-eyed, ambitious young person with a solid work ethic and the desire to do something cool with your life. Then before you know it, you're leaving multiple *Sorry I missed your birthday but we're doing a reeeaaaally big deal at work* voice mails, and only using initials in your e-mail signature (so annoying). How does this happen, you ask? Well, the more immersed you become in a given role, the greater the risk that you will lose track of your life outside of work–like Johnny Depp in *Donnie Brasco* or Lindsay Lohan in *Mean Girls*. In fact, both movies provide excellent frameworks for discussing Toolish transformations.

Though polar opposites on the surface (*Mean Girls* is a clever comedy that examines the trials and travails of high school popularity and backstabbing, while *Donnie Brasco* is a tough drama about an undercover cop who joins the mafia) the two movies are both built on the same "deep cover" plotline,* which is strikingly similar to how Toolish transformations usually play out in the working world. Take a look.

INTRO: BLINDED BY THE BLING

When you're young and restless, nothing is flashier than money. Making money, moving money, or sitting next to money can be intoxicating. For Donnie Brasco, money meant power. The fat money clips, luxury cars, and duffel bags filled with hundreds caused people to respect and fear him. Donnie developed a taste for power and authority, which caused a lot of problems in his marriage and skewed his sense of morality as well.

Cady Heron in *Mean Girls*, on the other hand, was blinded by the hot clothes, bags, and accessories that money can buy. Cady's designer bling turned her into a Paris Hilton–esque school socialite and earned her more than a few stares from guys and girls alike. She developed a craving for attention and pursued superficial glory at the expense of real relationships and her grade point average.

I am not out to suggest that money is evil. Not by a long shot. Furthermore, nothing is wrong with being excited or motivated by money, so long as you recognize that it can be intoxicating and addictive. Don't let cash consume you at the expense of all the other things that matter.

---

*Point of clarification: We are going to look at elements of the "deep cover" (or "undercover") genre, rather than the movie *Deep Cover* (starring Laurence Fishburne). That said, *Deep Cover* would fit appropriately as an example as well.

ACT 1: THE ACCEPTANCE GAME

No undercover operation truly gets off the ground until one gets accepted by his/her mark. In order to gain acceptance, one must show true commitment. For Donnie Brasco that meant proving that he was willing to get violent. For Cady it meant talking trash about her friends and teachers to show the "Plastics" that she could be a catty bitch. For a few investment banker friends of mine, it has meant proving their dedication to the firm by working longer hours than the characters on *Grey's Anatomy*.

The path to acceptance is very dangerous because in convincing your peers and superiors that you are committed, you run the risk of subconsciously convincing yourself that your unhealthy behavior is justified. As Cady says, "I know it may look like I've become a bitch, but that's only because I'm acting like a bitch."

ACT 2: LEGACY RELATIONSHIPS GET KICKED TO THE CURB

When you get in too deep, promises get broken, marriages crumble, and friends "don't even know you anymore." In deep cover movies, the relationship-buster scene signifies the point at which it becomes clear that the protagonist is in way over his head. Once he severs ties to people outside "the family," there's almost nothing to protect him from losing all perspective, and he officially becomes "one of them." The same thing happens during a Toolish transformation. Once you sever all ties with your friends—maybe you get in a fight with a buddy who calls you out for bringing your Blackberry camping or your girlfriend gets pissed because you rank her below your boss in your T-Mobile "Fave 5"—pretty soon you'll start spending your weekends tweaking PowerPoint decks because you find it more fulfilling than dealing with your former friends, who "just don't get it."

ACT 3: ALL PERSPECTIVE IS LOST

When I worked for a crazy start-up that had me flying all over the country every week, my entire sense of normalcy was thrown off. My hours were so nuts and the atmosphere got so intense (like many small companies, we were faced with a never-ending string of urgent crises) that I completely failed to sit back and notice that I had sacrificed my personal life for a job that wasn't really going anywhere. Furthermore, I didn't particularly like what I was doing, and the fruits of my labor hadn't provided me with any sense of accomplishment. Despite all of these red flags, I still found it very difficult to quit because I had been so involved for so long. Like Donnie Brasco, I was well aware that my organization had some major-league faults, yet still I was hesitant to abandon "the family." Long story short, I wasted nearly a year of my life treading water because I was in too deep to see it was time to get out of the pool.

CONCLUSION: THE TRUTH HURTS . . . BUT HOW BADLY?

Both *Donnie Brasco* and *Mean Girls* peak when the main characters come to the realization that their undercover roles are ruining their real-world lives. Cady's epiphany occurs just in time for her to snap out of her undercover funk and reclaim her pre-Plastic life. Donnie, on the other hand, never fully recovers. Though he gets pulled out of the underworld, he remains jaded and cynical and has an extremely difficult time adjusting back into the real world.

Don't let your professional identity take over your personal life. The story won't end happily. Besides, the whole deep cover genre is kind of played out.

PART TWELVE

Career-Limiting Moves

MOMENTARY (COL)LAPSES IN JUDGMENT CAN
HAVE LONG-TERM EFFECTS ON YOUR CAREER.

I'd like to take a moment to discuss the "code of conduct" (COC). Every organization has one. In the smallest, most informal organizations the COC may be communicated via a simple list of rules posted on the bathroom wall, or during a talk out back in which Dougie tells you not to "touch the cash register or talk about Mrs. Pachenko's muffin top." In contrast, large corporations will communicate their COCs by holding several mandatory, formalized training sessions, each of which focuses on a different ethical arena, such as "sexual harassment" and "diversity training." Having sat through sessions of Fortune 500 COC training myself, I can confirm that they are, in fact, dead boring. It's a lot like drivers ed, really. The sessions run 60 percent too long, most of the info taught is common sense, you watch outdated videos, and everyone (including the instructor) would rather be somewhere else. That said, I don't advise completely shutting off your brain during the slide shows, if only because the painful indoctrination of the golden-rule-based concepts will help you avoid making "career-limiting moves" in the future.*

Career-limiting moves (CLMs) are acts, behaviors, or statements that inhibit one's ability to achieve one's maximum potential in his or her career. CLMs are not generally performance-based mistakes. Rather they are avoidable, boneheaded, "What were you *thinking*?" moves. Postmortem analysis of a CLM usually reveals emotionally charged decision making (like telling your boss to "go @¢$% herself"), piss-poor external advice from a peer ("Dude, there's nothing wrong with padding your résumé with an extra graduate degree. It's not like anyone will check."), or just inexplicable moments of stupidity (piercing your tongue two days before a huge presentation). CLMs can seriously inhibit your ascent in a

---

*And sometimes they have tests at the end.

chosen profession or organization, so you might as well take steps to avoid them.

Given the impulsive nature of CLMs, there isn't a lot of advice I can give other than to look both ways before you cross the street. However, what I can do is offer up examples of CLMs from the pop culture world to help you avoid replicating mistakes made by others.

The Sauce

BOOZE IT AND LOSE IT, PARTNER.

KNOW, I KNOW. Inappropriate flirting and substance abuse are actually two separate career-limiting moves, but they hang out together so often that I figured I might as well just combine them. Besides, I've got an example that covers them both.

"Broadway" Joe Namath is one of the most celebrated quarterbacks in NFL history. In 1969 he guaranteed the Jets would win Super Bowl III and then delivered on his promise with a stellar performance. In addition to his performance on the field, he became an accomplished TV personality by guest-starring on several sitcoms, briefly hosting his own talk show, and announcing games on *Monday Night Football*. As he grew older, it seemed a foregone conclusion that America would remember Broadway Joe as an all-American hero. Then he got plastered and hit on Suzy Kolber on national TV.

During an on-camera interview in December 2003, Kolber, a sideline reporter for ESPN, posed the following question to Broadway Joe: "Joe, it's been a tough season for Jets fans. What does it mean to you to see the team struggling?"

Namath, who was visibly intoxicated at the time, responded by leaning his face toward Kolber and muttering, "I wanna kiss you," through his drunken, shit-eating grin. Did I mention that this was on national television?

An embarrassed Namath apologized the following week, claiming that the incident was a mess-up and he'd never do it again. Such is the case with CLMs. CLMs are usually one-time-only events, but you can never take them back. Joe Namath's brief dance with sexual harassment won't overshadow his stellar accomplishments on and off the football field. However, he now has a dash of "dirty old man" mixed into his "American hero" legacy.

Sex, booze, and work don't mix. That goes for office parties as well as the daily grind. Sure, there's nothing wrong with sipping a cocktail or two at a company-sponsored happy hour, but don't get tanked and unleash your inner sleaze, lest you risk permanently tarnishing your all-American reputation.

Amex Abuse

DON'T TRY TO CHEAT WITH RECEIPTS.

F YOU PLAN on keeping your job, I suggest that you refrain from spending company resources to construct a vodka-urinating ice sculpture of Michelangelo's *David* for your wife's birthday party. Sounds pretty straightforward, right? Unfortunately, former Tyco CEO Dennis Kozlowski never got that memo. Nor did Dennis think twice about commissioning a large birthday cake shaped like a naked woman, or flying in Jimmy Buffett (and entourage) to provide the entertainment for the same party . . . all on the company's dime. Did I mention the party was on the Mediterranean island of Sardinia? Sounds like one hell of a blowout and one hell of a career-limiting move. Not only did Dennis get fired, he also got eight to twenty-five years up the river.

Always play it safe with expense accounts. Your corporate Amex might call to you, but there's no reason to risk your career on an extra bottle of wine, hotel movie, or an ice sculpture that tinkles Stoli.

Cubicle Cross Fire

KEEP POLITICS OUT OF THE OFFICE.

WILL NOT WRITE about the Dixie Chicks. Initially I considered referencing the 2003 incident in which Natalie Maines (the lead singer) talked trash about George W. Bush on stage and immediately alienated half of the Chicks' fan base. I was going to mention how I found it amusing that the band initially tried to downplay the incident and then acted surprised when it caused their record sales to fall faster than Courtney Love at a cable awards show. Next, I was going to suggest that the next time Natalie wanted to tell a secret onstage, she should probably make the audience collectively pinky-swear not to tell anyone ... but I won't say any of that. You see, my wife told me that I would be stupid to write such nonsense because the Dixie Chicks did this whole documentary thing and went on *Oprah* and now their music is downloaded almost as much as that of those Chinese college kids who lip-synched to the Backstreet Boys. Even though half the country stations still won't touch them with fifty-foot antennae, they did win six Grammies in 2006, including one for "Not Ready to Make Nice," a song about the whole incident. Man, that could have been embarrassing for me. Phew.

Since I'm not writing about the Dixie Chicks, I'll keep this short and to the point: Don't talk politics at work, don't talk politics at work, and don't talk politics at work. Sorry to sound repetitive, but some people need a little extra nudge.

You don't really have anything to gain by talking politics at work, unless you work on Capitol Hill. More often than not, the only people who will take time out of their day to engage you in political conversation are those who vehemently disagree with you. There's no reason for you to go around picking fights when you're working. Save it for your blog, Limbaugh.

Talkin' Trash

NOBODY LIKES HANGIN' WITH HATERS.

WHEN **TERRELL OWENS** was hired as a wide receiver for the Philadelphia Eagles in 2004, his arrival was met with a mixture of anticipation and anxiety. On one hand, T.O. was one of the most gifted athletes in the NFL. His statistics with his old team (the San Francisco 49ers) were amazing and he hadn't shown any signs of slowing down. His presence would be sure to make the Eagles more dangerous on the field. Unfortunately, his presence on the team was likely to make the locker room more dangerous as well. T.O. had a rep for butting heads with his coaches, his teammates, and the media.

As it turned out, T.O. made good on both predictions. During his first (and only) full season in Philly, he caught fourteen touchdowns and helped guide the Eagles to the Super Bowl (they lost). Once the season ended, however, T.O. began calling out his teammates in public and talking trash about the Eagles' organizational brass. His unprofessional behavior led to a string of suspensions, keeping him off the field for more than half of the 2005 season. He was shipped out of town the following year.

Don't talk trash in the office (that includes mindless gossip). There really isn't any benefit, unless you are looking to make a name for yourself as a tight-pants villain in the world of professional wrestling.

Sweet Little Lies

ERGONOMIC CHAIRS WON'T HELP A BIT IF YOUR PANTS ARE ON FIRE.

N THIS CHAPTER, I'm going to revisit the exploits of several fab fabricators in order to highlight a few ways that lying can harm your career.

RELATIONSHIPS GET "FREY'D."

In 2005, James Frey's "memoir," *A Million Little Pieces*, became the hottest book in the country. The runaway success was largely due to the fact that Oprah selected *Pieces* for her book club in the fall of that year. Needless to say, the queen of daytime talk was none too pleased to discover that many of the million little details in Frey's book were completely made up. The next time James went on the show, Oprah got medieval on his ass.

When you lie about your work, you risk losing your relationships along with your credibility. The deeper you dig yourself into a lie, the more people you drag down with you. Your friends won't soon forget it.

IMAGES GET "ICE'D."

Nineteen-ninety was the year Vanilla Ice recorded "Ice Ice Baby," one of the first rap joints to become a Billboard number one hit. By 1991, however, America figured out that Vanilla didn't have nearly as much flavor as advertised. Turns out he had lied about his rough childhood and gangbanging past. Almost overnight Vanilla lost more street cred than Jared lost weight on the Subway diet. Nobody really listened to that white boy play his funky music after that. He was a pretty stellar character on the *Surreal Life*, though. . . .

While Vanilla Ice is pretty absurd (in general), his actions aren't uncommon in the working world. Shady people pad their résumés all the time, and it usually comes back to haunt them. In 2007 the dean of admissions at MIT was forced to resign because she admittedly misrepresented her credentials when she had initially applied to work at the school . . . twenty-eight years earlier. That's the thing about lying—you never know when your yarn will unravel.

FANS GET PISSED.

"Yeah right." That's what millions of American women collectively muttered after Angelina Jolie claimed she and Brad Pitt (then with Jennifer Aniston) hadn't been anything "more than friends" on the set of the 2005 spy flick *Mr. & Mrs. Smith*. That lie was so easy to see through that it might as well have been one of Angelina's costumes from *Gia*. How dumb did she think we were? By the time her quote hit newsstands, she and Brad had adopted half the UN together.

In retrospect, Angelina should have just come clean about her feelings for Brad, but she didn't. She chose to walk along a shady path instead, and as a result women in grocery lines from coast to coast were quick to label her as a "home-wrecking hooch."

If you get caught in a transparent lie, even your most loyal fans will be reluctant to forgive you. And unlike Angelina, you won't be able to retreat to Cambodia until the fury blows over.

Failure to Separate Church and Office

SAVE YOUR SERMONS FOR AFTER WORK.

IN 1992 SINÉAD O'Connor was one of the hottest female artists on the planet. Two years earlier her album *I Do Not Want What I Haven't Got* went platinum twice and her single, "Nothing Compares 2U," was an international smash. In October of 1992 the beautiful, bald songstress from Ireland appeared as the musical act on *Saturday Night Live*. For her first number, Sinéad performed the title track from her new album with a full band. For the second song, she chose to perform an old Bob Marley tune, "War," a cappella. Dressed in white and surrounded by candles, Sinéad was captivating. At the conclusion of the song, however, she pulled out a picture of the pope, held it up to the camera, and then ripped it in half while she encouraged the stunned audience to "fight the real enemy." Oh, snap!

While Sinéad's motives for ripping on/up the pope remain cloudy, the effect the *SNL* incident had on her career was clear as day. Sinéad's subsequent fall from grace was arguably the swiftest of the decade for anyone not named O.J. Simpson.*

---

*Standing trial for murder is most definitely a CLM, even if you get acquitted. Unless you're a rapper.

I believe in a strict separation of church and office. By no means am I intending to renounce or belittle the importance of spiritual or religious faith in everyday life. I'm just saying that work is not the place to proselytize. At best you will make a couple of your colleagues uncomfortable, and at worst you run the risk of alienating yourself from hordes of coworkers, clients, and customers. Don't believe me? Ask Tom Cruise.

The XXXtreme Makeover

WHAT EVER HAPPENED TO NICE, YOUNG JESSICA SPANO?

ALL APOLOGIES TO SHERYL Crow, but sometimes a change don't do you good, especially when that change is an abrupt, drastic, and ill-conceived image makeover. Just look at what happened to Liz Berkley.

From 1989 to 1993 Elizabeth Berkley was a small-screen queen. As Jessie Spano on *Saved by the Bell*, she was a role model for millions of young kids. Jessie was pretty, athletic, and extremely smart. She showed girls that brains were cool and drugs were bad (remember the "I'm so excited, I'm so excited . . . I'm so . . . *scared*" episode?). But in 1994, after shooting *Saved by the Bell: Wedding in Las Vegas* (a made-for-TV movie), Berkley felt it was time for a change. Like many young sitcom stars before her, she wanted to break away from her perky, kid-friendly TV persona and show off her range and flexibility as a mature actress. So for her next project Berkley tackled a very mature role aimed at a very mature audience.

In 1995 the movie *Showgirls* premiered to a universal chorus of boos and dirty snickers. Berkley played Nomi Malone, an aspiring showgirl who moves to Vegas to pursue her dreams but winds up in some extremely awkward positions. The role was dirty, man. I'm not talking "Christina Aguilera, a-little-dirty-but-still-really-talented," either. Liz Berkley went full-on Skinemax and the project bombed. Needless to say, America wasn't ready to embrace Jessie Spano as the star of a drawn-out soft-core music video. The transformation from Saturday-morning star to NC-17 minx was too abrupt to be believable, and Berkley's career has been haunted by *Showgirls* ever since.

I am not anti-change when it comes to professional images. I just think evolution is smarter than the XXXtreme makeover. For example, if you usually wear khakis and a button-down to work, don't show up on Monday flossed out like Dick Tracy. Forced image makeovers scream "Poser!" If you want to be viewed as mature and taken seriously at the office, let your work, as opposed to your look, do the talking.

A Final Word

'M NOT REAL big on closing statements, so I'm just going to wrap up with a brief summation:

Work hard.
Lose the ego.
Listen well.
Keep your eyes open.

Do these things (along with everything else you've just read, of course) and you will have a great shot at landing a good job and getting ahead once you're there. Just make sure that your zest for success doesn't drive you to start acting like an obnoxious Corporate Tool. Remember, there is a fine line between A-student and A-hole.

Appendix

TOOLISH TENDENCIES TEST: WHAT KIND OF CORPORATE TOOL *COULD* YOU BE?

The following quiz is not intended to determine whether or not you are, at this moment, a Corporate Tool.* Having just finished this book, you would undoubtedly pass such a test with flying colors (unless, of course, you were too lazy to read the whole book or you're a natural-born cheater). Instead, this little quiz is designed to identify where your "Toolish Tendencies" lie. In other words, what kind of Corporate Tool might you become should you cross over to the Dork Side? Not every Tool in the box looks alike.

---

*Not quite sure what a Corporate Tool is? Well maybe you should have read the rest of the book, you lazy pile. I'm not going to re-explain the concept now. What's that, you say? You're just flipping through the book at the store and you still haven't decided whether to buy it or not? Oh . . . well, I apologize for calling you a "lazy pile," but I'm still not going to explain the definition again. Go check out the intro.

The Quiz

Pick one answer per question. *Note: You may not like any of the answers listed. Tough. Just pick the one that looks most appealing.*

1. You're waiting in line to board a plane at the airport when your cell phone starts ringing. You
   a. answer it right away. It could be important and you're already wearing your Bluetooth headset.
   b. check to see who is calling then hit "ignore." It's not your boss, after all, and everyone else can wait a couple hours until you land.
   c. step out of line to answer the call, but quickly tell your mom that you are about to board the plane so you'll probably have to call her back.
   d. What phone call? Your phone has been off since you reached the airport. Why get stressed out before getting on a flight?

2. You roll to a close friend's dinner party the night after closing a huge client deal at work. You've been working on the pitch for weeks and your success positions you well for a promotion. Needless to say, you are fired up. You
   a. suppress your jubilation for a few hours. You wouldn't want to make everyone at the party jealous of your success.
   b. bring a bottle of expensive wine and insist that the group toast the client you've just signed.
   c. wait until someone asks you about work and then give them all the details. Your friends will be impressed that you didn't come out and tell them right away.
   d. reference the deal in passing at some point in the

evening, but purposefully downplay the importance of the event. It's just a little extra cash in your pocket. No big whoop.

3. Two weeks after starting a new job across town, what would your office walls look like?
   a. The walls would be filled with framed 8x10 action shots of you on vacation.
   b. Who cares? Maybe you'll get around to decorating in six months or so, if you feel like it.
   c. You probably have your company's most recent ad campaign framed and hanging next to your diplomas.
   d. You may have put up a framed Ansel Adams print, but you'll want to check out a few other company offices to figure out what's appropriate.

4. It's Monday. You and one of your colleagues are assigned to a two-week project that will have you working together round-the-clock. What are the odds that you'll be addressing her with a nickname by Wednesday?
   a. 0%. Some people don't like nicknames so why risk making her uncomfortable?
   b. 50%. Maybe if it's an obvious move, like Stephanie to Steph. But you probably won't bother to come up with a more personal or creative nickname.
   c. 75%. If her name has more than one syllable, she needs a nickname. Why waste time with excess pronunciation? You've got work to do.
   d. 100%. Everyone likes nicknames. In fact you may mix in two or three over the course of the project, just to keep her on her toes.

5. You've been tasked with assembling a group presentation for a company conference on Tuesday. It's 3 p.m. on Monday and one of your colleagues, Brandon, has been MIA all day. More important, he missed the noon deadline to submit materials for the presentation. You

    a. cut him out of the presentation. If he had a good excuse, you would have heard it by now.

    b. send him an e-mail letting him know he'd better get you something soon or else you'll have to tell the boss.

    c. wait another half hour before doing anything. Brandon probably had something important come up. You can always work late.

    d. don't worry about it. Your team understands how this presentation needs to run. It'll all work out.

6. Your boss invites you to play golf one Saturday. You are a wicked awesome golfer. Your boss played in high school but you can tell that she's not that good. Still, she is über-competitive and wants to wager a dollar on each hole. You

    a. crush her 16–2. She's the one who wanted to gamble.

    b. tank ten of the holes so that your boss pulls out a narrow 10–8 victory.

    c. tell your boss you're not into gambling on the course. You couldn't care less about what you score.

    d. suggest that the two of you just play "best ball" and try to break par as a team.

7. After lunch one day, you return to your desk to finish a report. As soon as you click on your e-mail icon, however, the

"Thong Song" starts playing at full volume. As you frantically scramble to mute the *"Thong Th-thong Thong Thong"* coming out of your speakers, everyone seated in your area cracks up, especially Dylan, the jackass down the hall. He obviously pulled the prank. Your boss shakes his head at you as he walks by. Your response?

    a. Dylan got you good, so you'll just give the man his props and get back to work.

    b. It's on like Donkey Kong. Dylan should expect to get creatively Punk'd every day for the rest of the week.

    c. These colors don't run, biyatch. Dylan needs to be taught a lesson and you'll probably be forced to take it up a notch (do something far more embarrassing to him) to ensure that he doesn't mess with you again.

    d. Don't even acknowledge anything happened. In fact, don't even acknowledge Dylan exists for the next week.

8. Your company splurges on hotel rooms for a convention in Vegas and you end up staying at the Bellagio. You're on your way back up to your room after dinner when none other than Donald Trump gets in the elevator with you. You

    a. introduce yourself and then ask his name, as though you were just meeting another run-of-the-mill guest in the elevator.

    b. tell him that you would have smoked the competition on *The Apprentice.*

    c. just look at the floor. You don't want to get caught ogling "The Donald."

    d. ask if it's cool to take a picture with your camera phone. The people at work would flip out.

9. Jessica, a senior executive at the company you've been with for five years, takes a job with a direct competitor in Cleveland. She e-mails you about a month later and asks if you would be interested in interviewing with her new group. The position would be similar to the one you currently hold. You would be most likely to

    a. "accidentally" delete the e-mail. You're fine where you are, so there's really no need to deal with the stress of talking to a competitor.

    b. wait a while to get back to her. Jessica hasn't gone out of her way to entice you, and if she wants you so badly, she'll offer something better.

    c. tell Jessica in no uncertain terms that you're not interested in any horizontal moves. If she had an offer that reflected a definitive step up the ladder, you'd listen.

    d. immediately let your boss know what's going on. You'll probably score some loyalty points and, recognizing that you're in demand, your boss might give your salary a nudge.

10. Your office is hosting a Friday happy hour at a bar downtown. You are most likely to

    a. show up late and then see if you can convince drunken colleagues to make fools out of themselves.

    b. grab a quick beer and leave. You don't want to be around when people get stupid.

    c. Jäger shots for everyone! Drink a few too many and close the place down.

    d. tell a couple friends to meet you there then share a bottle of wine (on the company) with them at a table in the corner.

Answer Key

1. Airport Call
   a. Hammer
   b. Drill
   c. Clamp
   d. Bagel Slicer

2. Dinner Party
   a. Clamp
   b. Drill
   c. Hammer
   d. Bagel Slicer

3. New Office
   a. Drill
   b. Bagel Slicer
   c. Hammer
   d. Clamp

4. Nicknames
   a. Clamp
   b. Bagel Slicer
   c. Hammer
   d. Drill

5. Presentation
   a. Drill
   b. Hammer
   c. Clamp
   d. Bagel Slicer

6. Golf with the Boss
   a. Drill
   b. Hammer
   c. Bagel Slicer
   d. Clamp

7. Thong Song Prank
   a. Clamp
   b. Hammer
   c. Drill
   d. Bagel Slicer

8. Trump
   a. Bagel Slicer
   b. Drill
   c. Clamp
   d. Hammer

9. Competitive Offer
   a. Clamp
   b. Bagel Slicer
   c. Drill
   d. Hammer

10. Happy Hour
    a. Drill
    b. Clamp
    c. Hammer
    d. Bagel Slicer

Results Explanation

Tally up your answers. If you earned six or more of any one tool then you should probably read the explanations below because you've got a dominant Toolish tendency.

Hammer: The classic Corporate Tool. You drink the organizational Kool-Aid with every meal. You're loyal till the end—if the boss says "pound," you say "how hard?"

Clamp: Guess what? You're a wuss. If your boss gets mad at you, you're likely to break out in hives. Everything at work causes you to stress, especially when deadlines are looming.

Drill: You're straightforward, aggressive, and you thrive on power. Your stance on life is "Hey, if they can't handle my intense style, they should have hired an ordinary screwdriver." Some call you "decisive"; others call you "dickhead."

Bagel Slicer: Aren't you just the coolest little tool that never lives up to its potential. When you were brought on, your boss was *so sure* that you would be a valuable, everyday contributor. In reality, though, you'd rather just hang out on the shelf with the martini shaker and talk about how "novel" you are.

All right, I'm done for real now. Get to work.

Acknowledgments

Without the following people, this book never would have happened:

Mom: Without you, I would have kept "productivity" and "happiness" separate. Thanks for being so supportive.

Dad: Without you, I wouldn't know how to tell a good story. I enjoy following in your footsteps.

Cara and David: Without you, I never would have had the courage to buck convention and do something creative. Throughout this process (and life) you have been brilliant co-conspirators.

The crazy clerk from the Days Inn in rural Georgia: *Without you, I might not have quit my job and given this project the attention it needed. Thank you for chasing off those "pesky teenagers" with your rake at 1:45 a.m., thus prompting me to consider making a change in my life.*

Roger Jellinek (my agent): Without you, I might be slinging books out of the trunk of my car. Thanks for teaching me the basics of the business and finding a great home for this project. You are as calm, cool, and collected as they come.

Sarah Rainone and **Talia Krohn** (my editors): Without you, this would be a totally different book. You are fantastic editors—funny, disciplined, thoughtful, and attentive. Thanks for answering every single one of my (daily) questions.

Roger Scholl: Without you, I might be one of those frustrated writers who view publishers as "the man." Thanks for giving me room to experiment.

Meredith McGinnis, Joy Dallanegra-Sanger, Carolyn Pilkington, Rachel Lapal, and Sonia Nash (at Doubleday): Without you, this project would have no legs. Thanks for contributing your time, your ideas, and your talents.

The people who invented cable television: *Without you, I would have very little material.*

Harry Beckwith: Without you, I would have had difficulty getting started. Thanks for offering your time, your expert eye, and your thoughtful feedback.

Christine Clifford Beckwith: Without you, I still might not have an agent. Thanks for sharing your enthusiasm and introducing me around.

Bob Hurley and **Angela Anello:** Without you, I never would have studied professional culture in the first place. Thanks for throwing me into the fire.

David Fisher: Without you, I might acknowledge obstacles.

Barry Simmons: Without you, I would have had to brainstorm by myself at coffee shops.

All of my friends, family, mentors, and colleagues who contributed time and ideas: Without you . . . I'm not even going to go there.

Roger *(my dog): Without you, I would have been pretty lonely in my office. Thanks for learning how to roll over while I had writer's block.*

Finally,

Sarah: You amaze and inspire me on a daily basis. It's no coincidence that I began writing this book after our honeymoon.

224